Striper Surf

Also by Frank Daignault:

Twenty Years on the Cape: My Time as a Surfcaster

STRIPER SURF

by Frank Daignault

The Globe Pequot Press

Chester, Connecticut

Photo on p. 208 appears courtesy Frank Woolner; p. 213, courtesy Charley Cinto. All other photos by the author.

Library of Congress Cataloging-in-Publication Data

Daignault, Frank, 1936-
    Striper surf / by Frank Daignault.
        p.   cm.
    ISBN 1-56440-027-1
    1. Striped bass fishing—Atlantic Coast (New England)
    2. Surf fishing—Atlantic Coast (New England) 3. Striped bass
    fishing—New Jersey—Atlantic Coast. 4. Surf fishing—
    New Jersey—Atlantic Coast.   I. Title.
    SH691.S7D35 1992
    799.1'758—dc20   91-30129
                                                CIP

Manufactured in the United States of America
First Edition/First Printing

❧ Table of Contents ❧

⇒ *Preface* ⇐

The purpose of this book is to teach surfcasting for striped bass. Because of the compelling and widespread interest in the striper surf and the recent recovery of the species, what is presented here is intended for use in the northeast from Maine to New Jersey, known as the "Striper Coast." It is thus a regional work addressing situations with which the shore fisherman night be confronted in the world's finest striper water. It is drawn from my thirty years of surf-fishing experience, twenty of those years as a fishing writer.

Our mission here is to inform and to entertain. A former student and teacher myself, I appreciate the importance of presenting knowledge in as palatable and pleasurable a way as possible if it is to be wholly absorbed and the student's interest is to remain constant. The information might stand upon its own merit, but the risk of losing one student—however small a percentage that might represent—is too great; moreover, the instructor has an obligation to uphold the charm of the written word to the high standards of that literature that has preceded him. For these reasons many "lessons" are supported with anecdotes in the sincere hope that the delight and feel of surfcasting permeates the information. Indeed, if the squid stink and salt spray ooze from these pages as you read, and if you experience a certain loss upon their completion, I will have done my job.

Cinch a belt around your oilskins, check your drag, and note the wind, and let's go surf fishing for striped bass.

≈ *Acknowledgment* ≈

Among these central Massachusetts hills, there is a headstone that marks the resting place of a dear and first friend. As fate would have it, there are still those who run their hounds nearby seemingly in tribute to his life-long love of New England forests and waters. Indeed, the music of baying hounds is fitting for a man who spent his life hunting and fishing, and it could be no more well deserved for a person who savored every moment, while thinking enough of it to pass on its rudiments to those he loved.

He taught me as a small boy the importance of fine breeding in a gun dog, bullhead fishing in spring, the nuances of well-drifted garden worms for brook trout, and the drama of a river striper putting a bend into a rod. These later proved to be among the greatest of his gifts, save life itself.

As the quintessential outdoorsman, he was a master of all the crafts needed to follow the seasons, probing emerald depths and gunning frosty meadows. But it was not mastery of the tools for which I owe him so great a debt. Rather, it is this inscrutable harmony with the natural world, which so few of us know, and to which so many remain oblivious, that was his greatest contribution to my youthful formation.

When waterfowl mark the pastel dawn of a new day, or a line tightens from the take, I am compelled to remember the source of this lifelong abiding heritage.

To Eugene Daignault (1901–1960). To Papa.

$\backsim$ Aura of the Surf $\backsim$

I n the face of the commonly accepted dictum that a boat fisherman will take ten times the fish of someone fishing the shore, I'm often asked why I fish the beach. It is a valid question that comes up all the time—never from real surfmen, only occasionally from boatmen and most often from people who either don't fish themselves or have only a passing interest. The answer is worth treatment.

A significant part of the surf's appeal lies in the basic, universally agreed upon fact that taking fish from the beach is more difficult. Comparisons between fishing from shore and from boats will probably always get some attention from thinkers as it always has in the past. Part of the problem is that for any comparisons to be made, the issue needs a yardstick, a means of measurement. Unfortunately, angling success has a nasty way of ending up being equated with numbers of fish caught. Many give too little attention to more subjective values like the more self-reliant skills employed in surf fishing as opposed to the more technical ones utilized in boats. Not that technology has bypassed surfcasting: There have been notable advances in casting reels, particularly with the introduction of spinning on this continent. Rod materials—tubular glass and graphite compositions—have refined our cherished distances. Monofilament and noncorrosive braid have greatly improved reliability and strength. But these, by comparison, are superficial refinements in what remains a primitive craft: hurling something from the shore into a sea that seems boundless in size.

Boats, on the other hand, cover great distances seaward with electronic navigation aids, spare engines, depth soundings, and sonar that pinpoint size, number, and location of gamefish. If they suffer from any curse, it is overmechanization. Anyone fishing from boats had better be part mechanic and part electronics technician. As a result, a dichotomy between boat fishing and surfcasting emerges: primitive basics versus technology. Few would argue that such differences exist, nor would they disagree with the notion that technology wins if the measurement lies solely with fish in the box.

Basic to any comparisons between surf and boat fishing is that third dimension, the distance from shore. The surfman constantly grapples with casting distances, probably more than necessary. Nonetheless, it is one's only means of dealing with the "out there," the third dimension. You can never put anything out or bring it back without physical effort, usually, but not necessarily, as far as your back and shoulders will deliver. Not that surfcasting calls for great strength, but when the casts begin to add up, it does call for endurance. The work ethic is alive and well in the high surf.

In my early, formative years as a surfcaster, I noticed that many of the regulars would laud another's success by remarking something like, "He deserves a good fish, works hard." One cannot ponder such remarks without considering that much of our society has unaccountably come to admire that which comes easily. As a result, some inappropriate societal heroes are held up before our young as examples to be emulated. Natural ability and God given luck get more attention than work, study, and the mind's potential, sending incorrect messages about the formulation of success. With mind-sets like these in place, who is going to walk out onto a beach and cast and retrieve until the sun rises?

In this northeastern region, surfcasting has largely come to mean fishing for striped bass. This is a highly predatory and difficult-to-catch species, particularly for the shore angler. While it is largely done at night, fishing the striper beach by day doles just enough isolated successes to bring the sport's most important premise into question. Thus, on top of all the disadvantages that surfcasters heap upon themselves, they must practice their sport during unnatural night hours. Think of it: You are voluntarily working hard for long hours without pay during that little time when you are not earning a living or caring for a family . . . without sleep!

When we cast a meager offering that is scant inches long into a boundless sea, what will be there to take it? Where are the fish? Are we fishing wrong among a mother lode of stripers? Or are we fishing right in a place where the nearest catchable fish is miles away? Worse, we could be fishing wrong where there is nothing anyway. We have no sophisticated devices to draw neat little lines on graph paper so that we may separate the elements of success—technique versus location. We cannot change our bait or lure because of some certainty that fish are there. Any conclusions about what is in the foam-edged mystery in our fore are drawn from the most primitive forms of observation. We listen for the subtle pop of a break that is made amid the thunder of a booming surf, we sniff air that is diluted by an onshore gale, and we seek traces of bait washing up in darkness. Our skills are no different than those of our ancestors who sniffed and grunted a millennium ago. The only time we know we are doing something right is when we slide a brute onto the beach.

As prisoners of an ideology, surfmen have always claimed the shore as a stronghold of rugged individualism. Done right, the activity taxes the body and requires good sense as well as an understanding of one's natural surroundings. Surfcasting, then, should never be a head down, shoulder to the stone, hard work for work's sake: It should be a miserly conservation of energies. If a thousand casts must be made, make them upon a beach that has been read for bars, sloughs, and holes. Any tiderip tested high should be fished deep as well. If we are to endure the midwatch, we must decide when to save our strength as well as when to burn it.

For all the hard work, the enemy is boredom. There will always be periods when the nights defy separation in the mind. Such periods erode confidence and give way to care-

lessness. A great striper, weeks in the coming, takes at the very moment that you slap a midge from your arm. When will your next chance come?

No sport is without its own romance. For all that is said about odds stacked against the beach, the shore has its advantages. Along with being primordial in terms of what you must have to go fishing, it is a far safer place to take on an often unforgiving sea. For that reason you see more family fishing, where everyone—down to the smallest youngster in the tribe—gets his feet wet when stripers are punishing bait in the wash. Weather can be a deterrent, yet it only rarely makes things unsafe for the family. Short of a hurricane, fishing goes on.

The sweet song of a high surf creates a state of mind rich with anticipation. A making tide where swells clap over bars under shimmering moonlight can so raise expectations, or someone downtide with a good fish on the beach can make you think there have to be more. In your mind you know the drag is right, that the line is new, and that the hooks are sharp. Shoulders and hands function on their own, long past having to be told what will tempt a strike. But it is not until the line lifts from a violent take that mind and body truly come together. When the fish is on the shore, a mix of pride and excitement consummates all the planning, all the preparation, all the anticipation.

That is the way it is supposed to be.

PART ONE

LOCATING STRIPERS— WHERE AND HOW

Reading the beach is what takes the guesswork out of finding stripers.

⇒ Reading the Beach ⇐

Any time we embark on a hunt, it is imperative to have an intimacy with both the quarry and its environment. We deal elsewhere with striper behavior and examine at length the varied forms of "structure" where bass might be found. Here we look at the beaches themselves and our perception of how stripers use them.

The term "reading" no doubt comes from trying to determine the topography of the ocean's bottom, whether we can see it or not. Places that have more pronounced structure, where bars and trenches are visible from the outside, present a clear picture to the skilled and experienced eye. On the other hand, deep-water beaches, or shores where tidal exchange is slight, often have obscure bottom configurations that either cannot be read or must be assumed, based upon the shape of the land above. For instance, a large bowl-shaped washout along the beach implies a more active surf and set of current circumstances capable of creating such a washout. The chances are that such an indentation of the shore continues below the surface and, at the same time, presents evidence of more active currents. Certainly, if we cannot fine desirable structure, we have to seek out those elements that create it. It is a case of seeing as much of the bottom configuration as we can.

I can draw from memory one notable example, among many, to illustrate the influence of structure upon the behavior of striped bass.

Pochet Hole is the first good-size washout to appear on Cape Cod's Nauset Beach as one drives south from the access. It changes from time to time—an accident of the total meteorology of the passing seasons—but the long-term effects of local currents keep Pochet Hole a viable striper hot spot. One year there was a bar configuration there that was a classic example in extremes of readable beach topography.

The hole was gouged deep enough for about 200 yards along the shore and 100 yards seaward to present emerald coloring even at low tide. Bars paralleling the beach fell short of meeting at the hole's outside center by 50 yards, keeping 300 degrees of the hole closed at low tide. Structure alone gave the spot promise, but this particular day the indentation was filled with blueback herring—appearing as highly mobile dark patches—that were balled in scattered pods within its confines.

Lured by the magnetic appearance of the structure there, we were casting from the outside bars in full daylight when we noticed huge stripers cruising around the opening, sometimes following our plugs into the shallow surf. Later, with a rising tide driving us back to the dry beach, these moby linesides came into the hole to drive the bluebacks against the shore, where they lashed at them—as well as our plugs—in the first wave. All through the blitz I could not dispel the feeling that stripers had decided to move upon the bluebacks while their "trapping" opportunities were still good.

The Pochet example recalls a number of beach-reading considerations worthy of mention. During any daytime scouting you should always have a eye peeled for bait. Often this will appear as darkened patches of indistinguishable material that might even look like a patch of weed. Naturally, you need every viewing advantage possible, and polarizing glasses can immeasurably enhance the ability to visually penetrate the surface glare of the sea. Polaroids eradicate the sheen of the water's surface while displaying the subtle changes in shade that might be either bait or changes in depth. We would have never known of the cache of bait at Pochet, nor of the "followers" on the outer bars there without them.

In places where there is nothing apparently readable, one must note any observable differences, however slight. On the Rhode Island south shore is a 200-yard bottom of "cobblestone" arbitrarily placed upon 4 miles of otherwise sandy bottom. Stripers are not always there, but if fish are in the vicinity it is a better place to start than any other.

On many stretches of shore, it is difficult to relate bits of suitable structure we find to something nearby so that they may be marked. Some surfmen indicate favored locations by implanting bits of driftwood in the beach; however, there is a risk that these might be found and utilized by others.

The key to choosing the best places to fish is change, that is, finding any obstruction in the shoreline that might cause a passing striper to pause either in the search for feed or to utilize that obstruction to trap or pen bait fish. The corner where a jetty meets the beach is a suitable example, or there could be a section of boulder-strewn shore acting in the same way. Even an island can create a subtle speeding of tidal action along the adjacent shoreline. A point of sand jutting seaward would also be evidence of heightened tidal activity.

Thus, a clear relationship develops in our mind between structure and current, which become mutually dependent, and both appeal to foraging gamefish. Current creates structure, and structure implies the presence of current. Once it is noted that these exist, it then often becomes a case of determining which tides will lure bass into feeding position. Now, as the beach-reading craft comes into play, it is not only a case of *where* but *when*. After you read the section on night fishing, you will see that we can hastily reduce twelve or more hours of the day for determining when to fish a particular location.

Sandy shorelines that are replete with outer bars, holes, and trenches can be both appealing to stripers and a joy for the practice of beach reading. One can envision predators swimming a bar edge until they reach an opening, then passing through that opening to search out the depths of a hole for bait fish; we can also imagine bait being trapped in that hole so that a supply of forage remains in place, causing the larger killers to linger and feast upon them. Often such conditions are greatly dependent upon tide, because flooding water will cover this structure so deeply as to minimize the bottom configuration's influence; conversely, at low tide so much of the structure is exposed that only the most extreme portions of the total structure are valid.

To compound the influence of timing, stretches of coast that are gardens of bars, holes, and trenches tend to share the number of available gamefish. For example, one hole along the beach in 5 miles of shore narrows the options of both stripers and their antagonists, but a similar length beach with twenty nice-looking spots either has the linesides spread or divides one's chances of choosing the right one. This business of reading the beach is only easy when it works.

In our repeated reference to the hard work of surfcasting, perhaps not enough is made of doing so with enhanced efficiency. Blind, shoulder-against-the-wheel bullheaded effort with a thousand casts will never stand against a hundred made in well-read water.

INLETS

Any examination of the striper coast's most classic hot spots would show that their most recurrent quality is that they are also inlets. Knowledgeable stripermen have always known that inlets possess two qualities that draw stripers: current and foraging opportunities.

The most dramatic exchange of water takes place at inlets, which are the openings to bays, rivers, and other estuarine ponds. These not only furnish the moving water but contain a mother lode of bait fish that attract hungry gamefish. It is mandatory that those fishing such spots have an intimacy both with tide (see Tide section, pages 25–29) and its influences upon that particular inlet. All are different, the variables too complex to enumerate here, but an excellent starting point (dare we generalize?) would be to fish the inlets on the dropping tide. Then, while you are muddling through your first nights, the fine points of a new location begin to present themselves; for instance, even though the chart says that the tide is high, you'll notice that the water keeps running in long after that time. This is also true of water falling after low tide. The reason for this "lag" is the restriction at the opening of the inlet preventing the water from filling the backwater. As long as sea level is higher than the back estuary, inward flow will continue, in spite of an ebbing tide in front. Thus, slack water at an inlet, whether it is slack low or slack high, is always different, later, from that of the sea in front. The difference varies, both from one such opening to another and according to the moon phase, which governs the amount of water in exchange.

Sharpies who know their inlet can tell you precisely when slack will occur. They make a point of knowing this not only because it can signal the end of drift fishing on a falling tide, but because it is a magic interval in most inlets, when fish that have been holding in feeding position are most likely to cruise in search of bait or another feeding position in anticipation of tide change. It is a good fishing time, and they want to know precisely when it will occur, so that they are not caught with a can of beer in their hand when the place momentarily explodes.

We emphasize that dropping tides have elevated inlet fishing to our most opportune choice of structure. This is because estuaries served by inlets are the growing places and breeding grounds for much of the available forage; or, the forage finds its own food-chain opportunities within the estuary. Should this forage leave, it will characteristically take advantage of the outgoing tide or be swept up in it. In addition, currents—inlet size depending—reach out into the open sea, drawing attention to themselves. Such rips appeal to all foraging gamefish, stripers no exception; moreover, there is a significant temperature differential between the sun-heated backwater estuary and open water.

Falling water acts as an excellent conveyance for a bait or lure, permitting it to be "fed" seaward with an open bail or spool, often until the spool is empty. This "drifting," as it is sometimes called, is best served by a floating swimming plug to avoid hanging the bottom. Long drifts produce, but one can probe a variety of eddies by varying the length of line tossed to the currents. Plugs can also be permitted to drop back in the current more slowly, drumming as they go. A live eel, alewife, or bunker can be live-lined in the current, as long as it is unencumbered by a sinker. Feel your way, and never let large quantities of line tumble from your spool unless you're sure the bait is drifting; otherwise, the meat is out 100 feet, the line 400. Such baiting works more often as it drifts freely seaward, where a plug requires the resistance of line to make it swim.

Because there is nothing secret about inlet fishing, you will find other surfmen at most inlets. For this reason your method should be in harmony with what others are doing. Never drift bait in a crowd of pluggers where currents are heavy: The technique is slower and can cause the fouling of lines.

Except for a brief period at slack tide, bottom fishing is usually impossible in most openings. Inlets that have milder currents, or at current edges if crowds permit, can be baited with beefed-up sinkers to intercept stripers headed for feeding. Keep in mind that some inlet bottoms are junkyards that foul a sinker quickly, and current enhances that possibility.

Many inlets have a more favorable side that provides better fishing. This inconsistency can be caused by structure, wind direction, tide phase, and even accessibility. Choices are simple when access is limited to one side; however, if choices are permitted, I like being inside the "hook" of current. Let me explain.

On a calm night you can often see the lines of infusion reaching out from the beach, then curving with the ocean's tide; thus, if an inlet is running east and the sea tide is running south, these infusion lines will hook to the south. After tide chart low the hook will turn to the north. Even though water continues out of the inlet, the change in sea tide—hooking first one way then the other—explains why so many inlets change sides in angling importance while you're fishing. Any change is important because it forces gamefish into better feeding positions. Unlike some bland, nameless spot along the beach, in a six-hour period an inlet's deck is shuffled four times: slack, dropping with a left hook, dropping with a right hook, and another slack.

While falling water is the standardized timing of inlet fishing, many yield better or equally well during a rising tide. They certainly enjoy less attention from other anglers during this period. When nearby beaches have a good bait supply, that forage often passes through the gates of inlets and—considering currents—bass will lurk in these currents to grab what passes. In the case of larger openings, bass often move through on the rise to go in and pass again during the drop.

Sea openings that are kept from growing wild by the construction of flanking jetties (see section on Jetties, pages 14–20) change little, but others are always on the move. The locations of channels and bars lie at the whim of wind and sea, forcing you to practice reading of the water from time to time. Some inlets creep along in the same direction until they close. Then local authorities come along with a bulldozer to rescue trapped marine life and keep the pond from going stagnant. The event is usually the worst-kept local secret, since grapevines of regulars inform one another of the impending angling boom. There are probably more closed-over estuarine ponds opened in May than any other month.

Having seen some of these ponds opened, I've watched eels denied access to their sea spawning scurry for the opportunity while alewives were practically bumping heads with them to gain access to inland spawning beds. Meanwhile, opportunistic linesides cashed in on the event. Without the heavy equipment, many great fish and great surfcasters might never have met.

How far does one stretch application of the inlet concept? The Cape Cod Canal is an inlet, I suppose, though admittedly of a magnitude beyond what we've covered here. Some of the so-called staging areas are really oversized inlets that rally currents, offer feed, and hold great striped bass. Race Point guards the opening of Cape Cod Bay; and a rip line stretching from Montauk to Fisher's Island marks the entrance to Long Island Sound. Small wonder that these places are so dear to the hearts of surfcasters.

Thirty years ago, when a small group of us played poker and drank beer at a local watering hole, we used to rally around Johnny Koback, who talked of stripers with his arms outstretched. We used to love to hear him romanticize about the striper surf and 40-pounders screaming braid from a squidder amid his incantations of God-given rewards for night on night midwatch hunts for striped bass. Gathering amid the smell of stale beer and sawdust while the snow swirled past frosted windows in the deep New England winter, we promised ourselves that we would someday taste the salt and experience this alluring love affair of which he so often spoke.

Then one of the gang, fully knowing that none of us knew the first thing about finding stripers, asked:

"Johnny, if there is one thing we should know to catch stripers, what is it?"

And Johnny, sweeping a section of the well-varnished bar clean, dipped a finger into his beer drawing a wet line of shore, a circle on the inside, and an opening to connect them.

"Look for falling water," Johnny admonished. Pounding the bar with his finger tip like the impatient mentor that he was, he said, "The bait comes out here! The fish lay here! What could be easier?"

Then, as if trying to show that he meant no serious condemnation, he ordered a round for us "wet-behind-the-ears" surf fishermen. Not a bad beginning for somebody who would like to find stripers.

ESTUARIES

We have treated the ocean and inlets as viable places to seek stripers, and we would be remiss if we overlooked the inside of those inlets.

An estuary is a tidal arm of the sea or the lower course of a river. From that we can elaborate upon two significant considerations: Estuaries are tidal, and they often contain variable quantities of fresh water. Moreover, broadly stated, there are no size limitations on them; an estuary can be as large as Chesapeake Bay or the Hudson River—both breeding grounds for dominant races of striped bass—or as small as a five-acre pond connected by a trickle of flow to open water.

Estuaries are the nurseries of many of the forage species of nearly all our marine gamefish. As a consequence these productive ecosystems offer increased feeding opportunities for all predators, the striper but one example of many that rely upon them.

It would be outside the bounds of this book to elaborate on the degradation of estuaries since the arrival of modern man. On the other hand, we should emphasize that the reason estuaries have been so overutilized is that they provide safe harbors for shipping, harvesting of shellfish, and less hostile environments for coastal dwellers. Cities have sprung up on our coast's most utilitarian estuaries, fouling them with pollutants and choking off the life blood of the sea a result. Enough said.

Naturally, the same lure of opportunity that brings bass to an inlet will bring them inside an estuary. Depending upon the size of such waters, the fish may even stay during the day to lounge in deeper sections. As a highly mobile and opportunistic gamefish, the striper may also move through an inlet under cover of darkness in the smaller tidal ponds only to return to deeper water offshore by daybreak. Estuary size and available water cover will determine whether it remains.

Larger estuaries are certain to hold linesides somewhere within them around the clock. Moreover, their initial appeal—feeding opportunities—is likely to induce this tendency to stay nearby. But fish are not going to take up residence unless the forage base is the best they can find. In the spring, when feeding opportunities are their lowest in the sea, estuaries seem to have more to offer. In my early years as a striperman, I marveled at how poor the fishing would be along the beach each spring and how productive it was for the larger bass in the quiet tidewaters during the deep night. Of course the reason was that alewives were on their spawning run, no doubt leaving an alluring scent trail the full dis-

As these Narragansett Bay surfcasters can testify, estuaries provide a forage base that draws stripers from the open sea.

tance from the open Atlantic to the sweet-water river or brook of their birthplace.

Similarly, a run of menhaden (pogies) will draw stripers up into a bay to cash in, but these arrive later in the year, say July, and depart in autumn. During these months, however, what with all forage in the midst of its annual expansion, feeding opportunities elsewhere create a greater dispersal of stripers than that which occurs in spring. But not all estuaries host an alewife run, nor are all bays attractive to pogies. This points up the need to know as much about locating bait fish as about locating stripers: frequently one and the same.

There is no "surf" in the protected waters of an estuary; thus, the feel of fishing this kind of water can easily be likened to fishing a lake or river. This is so much the case that many anglers tend to dangerously downgrade the strength of their equipment in response to the notion of catching smaller fish, but these waterways are connected to the same ocean with the same potential.

For fly fishermen these waters provide an opportunity to wade and cast without the nuisance of surf tugging at their stripping and having to deal with breakers forcing them away from the water. Bait depending, the fly often provides a better opportunity to simulate the smaller bait fish of salt ponds. Serious fly fishermen adapting to the salt chuck would be advised to begin in such tidewaters.

Probably the strongest case for estuarine fishing lies in the chance to fish when it is impossible elsewhere. In a given year there can be any number of storms that will ruin all opportunity for coastal fishing. You can't fish the beach when 20-foot boomers are curling white ¼ mile out, and you won't fish it until the scud, mud, silt, and weed have settled, which is often days. But your bay- and river-fishing counterpart hasn't missed a cast and if he knows what he is doing and when to do it, he may even be logging some moby linesides in the process.

When I feel like fishing—and Lord knows that is most of the time—I don't want anybody or anything to be able to stop me.

JETTIES

Those piles of stones that reach out into the sea have a purpose. Their mere existence is neither an accident of nature nor is their location arbitrarily selected. Jetties have two purposes: to prevent beach erosion and to protect inlets from closure by an ever-active sea that is always shifting sand to places where it is not wanted. In many cases, were it not for jetties, most inlets would eventually close up, then starve valuable estuaries of their necessary exchange of seawater. When this happens marine life loses access to the sea, the water loses salinity, and shellfish, usually part of the local economy, die off.

Consequently, many jetties flank important inlets, acting as delightful surfcasting platforms. In Rhode Island every jetty I know of has this purpose. It is also a worthwhile digression to point out that Rhody refers to most of its jetties as "breach-ways," because the rockpile's purpose in that state, in all instances, is to retain the "breach" in the shore to sustain the estuary it serves.

The nuances of jetty fishing are wholly different from those of the beach. Rarely is there any wading, yet for the most part, waders are worn for splash protection. Depending on the rock pile, the structure of the stone placement can be dangerous, offering yawning spaces between them that a careless angler can fall into and likely sustain injury. Nights when there is little sea running, there is a temptation to get closer to the water, where lower forms of marine life grow on the rocks and render them as slippery as ice. On big-water nights the foamers roll in, then explode, sending cascades of water upon anglers, soaking them at best or sweeping them off the rocks at worst. Just how great the risk is depends upon weather, the angler's skill, and judgment. Overall few deaths or permanent injuries occur on jetties; but then, those I've known who fished them had an all-abiding respect for what they were doing. They were also skilled at dealing with the two problems of getting around safely and staying dry.

Good wading equipment is not necessary here, as you will rarely be standing in green water. Hip boots covered with a pair of oilskin trousers or splash pants cover most situations. These can be supplemented at times with a foul-weather top with a hood or a sou'wester hat. A person who knows the stones can usually get around well without any special footwear. Many pros have corkies on their feet or spikes, however, to deal with the darker rocks, which have marine growth that can be as slick as a viscosity meter. I have nothing bad to say about any of this equipment. But an overlooked option that has never taken hold in surf fishing are the stocking-foot waders and wading shoes so widely used by freshwater-river anglers.

Having purchased this gear originally for trout and salmon fishing, it was a simple matter for me to give it a try in the salt chuck. Here is what I learned: Warmer months stocking-foot waders, which weigh only a few ounces, are both cool and lightweight; they cost less than conventional waders and last longer. My wading shoes, which are equipped with felt bottoms, deal best with the slick rocks. Indeed, the footwear is akin to equipment intended for mountain climbing, a situation somewhat mindful of many jetties. While my waderclad counterparts are tripping and sliding, encumbered by the weight and bagginess of their surfwear, I can move about as though I were not dressed for it at all. I must caution you, though: The same arrangement on a sandy beach will have you cursing me until these pages yellow. The action of the surf has a way of slipping sand between your shoe and wader, cramping your toes, subtly adding to the weight of your footwear, and damaging the stocking-foot wader in time. The uniform I advocate is for jetties only.

Current ought to be the main consideration for those hunting for gamefish along the shore. Jetties are a sign of current, or they wouldn't be there. Consequently, I would begin fishing an area by examining its jetties very closely at all stages of tide. There is no better starting point. And never make the mistake of thinking that the dropping tide is necessarily always the best period to be fishing.

Methods for fishing jetties are no different than those that work for you in the usual striper surf. Whether plugging, livelining, or using bait on the bottom, it is a case of how well things are working in a given locale, the intensity of current, the type of bottom, or the bait that has gamefish there in the first place.

One challenge to jetty fishing—landing the fish—makes surfcasting from them a wholly different game. Let me draw you a picture:

The large granite slabs stretch out 300 feet from the beach in a pair that flank an inlet. During full tide the sea rushes between the jetties to the inside, a large estuary that is surrounded by a grassy salt marsh lush with small marine life—crabs, mummies, sand eels, immature winter flounder, American eels, needlefish, snapper blues, a few varieties of mollusks. It is a place where everything is after everything. In spite of the neat placement of the stones at the shore end, rocks on the outside end are battered and displaced so that it is impossible to position yourself for fishing. There also is a heavy surf running most of the time, and you could never stay there, because the water is too pushy and the stones covered with a slippery black moss. You are forced to stay on top of the jetty, 5 feet above the water at high tide and 10 feet at low. Despite this each wave sends high into the air a wall of harmless foam that can soak any surfcaster who is not wearing full waterproofing. How are you going to get the fish up?

It has always surprised me that many otherwise intelligent surfmen can plan a night at the shore, sleeping listlessly the night before in anticipation, have the ability to deliver miles of good casts end to end and to fish with impeccable equipment, but can overlook that little detail. The landing of the fish, after all, is the consummation of the sport's purpose. Yet, time after time, I have seen competent surfmen lose a fine striper or blue at the final moment, reaching for it in desperation, when a wave came crashing down upon them at some dangerous foothold. True, if we are to accept the rigors and precepts of surfcasting, disappointment belongs at the head of a long list, but bad planning or no planning at all is all too often an unnecessary cause of failure.

First, have a couple of places picked out ahead of time where a very large striper (these present the most serious problems) can be landed. Such places should be easy to climb down to at a given stage of tide. Have alternate landing sites that take sea conditions into account. In other words, know the stones. Even with such ideal spots embedded in the memory, you are going to need a sharp long-handled gaff, say 6 to 10 feet long. Keep it covered with a section of rubber tubing for safety. For an example we'll select as a likely size striper one of 40 pounds, which is attainable for the average surfman and not outlandish or too much of a long shot.

The fish has been hooked, line has been traded on the drag, and you can tell that it is ready to be led to your preselected landing sight. Using care with the light so as not to unduly spook the tired lineside, you climb down easily, lift the gaff, and feel the weight of the fish as the steel finds its mark. After hand-over-handing the gaff handle, you are able to grasp your catch by the gills. It's yours. How are you going to get back up onto the top of the rock pile?

You have a surf rod in one hand, 40 pounds of struggling striper in the other, your flashlight in your mouth, and a cramp is developing in your jaw. Worse, you are down 6 feet from safety, and you have a back-of-the-mind suspicion that the waves you have encountered so far have been a little lower than those coming. The only thing you are certain of is that you are not going to let go of that fish! It would help if you have a partner to pass the rod to, but what if you are alone? Moreover, even if you free a hand, the climb, now 40 pounds heavier, is not going to be that easy.

Then there is the question of the competence of anyone who might be around to help. It might surprise you how few people can be of any help in a situation demanding exact, unhurried movements that will get that fish up to a safe spot. You don't want somebody who is going to scramble from an incoming foamer leaving your bass to languor, unreachable, in a crevice among the stones. If you want to be certain that it is done right, you will have to do it yourself, and that can be easy.

I have never fished a jetty without an 8-foot section of ¼-inch nylon line tucked into my waders. Have a loop with an

Jetties offer prominent fishing spots, often flanked by striper-laden currents.

8-inch opening tied in advance. The rope can be released with one motion, then dropped through the mouth and out the gills, the end run through the loop. You can start the climb with a loose piece of rope in one hand, leaving the rod behind with its tip roughly where you expect to reach the top. This way you have two hands to climb with, and there isn't even the weight of a fish, which is still in the surf, to hamper your escape. It can all be done within seconds. Once out you can even option to haul your rod out first; the striper isn't going anywhere.

Jetties are widely known to be prime producers of worthwhile surfcasting. For that reason you are not likely to find much solitude. In fact, they can be very crowded at times. Unless being with the gang is an important aspect of the sport for you, you will be wise to learn what others are overlooking. For instance, many inlet flanking jetties enjoy more popularity on the dropping tide. I know one where casters line up, moving through three positions on the end, where each rock or position has an assigned function: Cast from number three; feed line from two; close your bail or clutch and swing from one. Surfmen on number 1 have an open path to the beach, where they do their fighting if they hook up. Sounds a little militant and overly regulated, but it is what is needed if everyone there is going to enjoy a fair and effective opportunity to fish the place.

Fishing opportunities at that gaggle of stones are only a fraction as good on the rising tide, but the caster who fishes there at the "wrong time" is alone, thus spared any lost time. Consequently, a sixty-minute hour of poorer fishing may be, in the long run, more productive than a ten-minute hour during the better fishing times.

There is an almost unlimited variety of things you can put to work for yourself, following the above example of being out-of-step to attain solitude. Jigging deep when everybody is plugging; using a canoe to reach an otherwise inaccessible side of a pair of jetties; fishing way inside to avoid the crowds that tend to gather at ends. It is a matter of being observant and acquiring some experience, because nothing in this surfcasting game comes easily. You are not going to learn how to get around on a jetty, how it is fished, and where it is being overlooked in one night. On the other hand, there is a sense of satisfaction that comes from being able to practice the craft with an original flair, especially if what you do is catching fish when others can not.

ROCKY SHORES

Much of what we have covered in reading sand beaches and jetties is applicable to rocky shores. Prominent points, indentations, or larger coves act either as places that command more water or where linesides can trap bait. It is the nature of these stony shores to be much more resilient to weather, more easily read from the viewpoint of "reading a beach," and more permanent as coastal structures.

Indeed, rockbound sections of shoreline—as can be found in Newport or Narragansett, Rhode Island; Montauk; and certainly the coast of Maine—harbor an abundance of bait and marine flora, which can act as both a hiding place for forage and a viable place for stripers to seek them, all good reasons why southerners call our fine species "rockfish."

As we saw with the jetties, there are complications in fighting and landing big linesides where stones can sever or damage a taut line in seconds. Even with a stout line, it is no easy chore to get close to a great fish on slippery rocks, often high above the water, with a booming sea throwing foam and green death at you. Worse, the delightful nooks and crannies that so appeal to bait and brought Mr. Striper there in the first place are now ideal for him to sulk in while rubbing at the thing in his jaw that so antagonizes him. There is a place in Narragansett where big stripers are famous for running in on a surfcaster's feet, then diving to bury the line in 5-foot strands of kelp. Many great fish have been lost there.

Let me share a concern that I have lamented all my life: Surfcasters always have fished with line and tackle that is way too light for stripers. For most people the average tackle with the average striper works out fine, and that is the trap in it. What of the above-average striper? The dream striper? This tackle might be suitable on some sandy beach that is without obstruction or hazard, but it *won't* be on the rockbound shores we describe here.

Whatever your choice of tackle, have a suitable place selected for landing a good fish, and make your timing for

Rocky shores can yield great stripers, but watch yourself—slippery rocks can be treacherous.

going down for him crisp, because there are few places more dangerous for surfcasters than these rocky shores.

Which brings us to an important consideration: Rocky shores kill surfcasters. In a lifetime of reading Rhode Island newspapers and fishing Narragansett, a typical rocky shore where surfmen enjoy the striper surf, I've noticed a death rate of roughly one per year. This is probably the most dangerous rate per mile of any stretch of shoreline on the Striper Coast. Characteristically, the fish are in, there is an onshore east or southeast wind, and the poor fellow had a good reason for going down too close. Right below the high-water mark, the stones are black, clear indication of marine growth, and it is as slippery as ice! Once you are in the water, your only chance is to swim seaward and hope that help makes it to you before you tire. This is not a pleasant alternative to being bashed to death on a rockbound shore by an unrelenting surf. I've made a few mistakes on the beach, but one error in judgment of the stones would have been my last.

≈ Tide ≈

J ust often enough to underline its importance, from time
to time people ask what tide is best for fishing in salt
water. It is one of those questions that doesn't really have
an answer, because the question lacks specifics. Indeed, such a
generalized question would only evoke a generalized answer,
if any at all. No generalization can be made about "best tide"
without tying it to a specific location. Only then does the
issue of tide begin to take on meaning.

At many locations tide is not a factor at all in the produc-
tivity of the fishing. This is particularly true of long stretches
of beach where the movement of water is not impeded or in
areas of the coast where the tidal exchange is slight. This
brings us to a critical factor in the discussion: tidal exchange,
the difference in depth between low and high tide. Generally
speaking, and there are other factors, the farther we get from
the equator, the greater the exchange. This is why we hear so
much about the great tides in the Maritimes, which are in and
of themselves quite natural but seem strange to us because of
the small tides that we are used to in the Northeast. For instance, Rhode Island's extreme tides are a shade over 4 feet.
Yet, for all purposes at the same latitude, Cape Cod has 11
feet. We are thus inclined to consider the Cape to produce far
more dramatic tiderips than Rhode Island. This is not to say,

however, that stripers are going to move miles and miles merely to have their flanks stroked by moving water. What we are saying is that if water is to move at all its influence can often be a consideration as to when we ought to be fishing. We hasten to add that tide is more important where its exchange is greatest. Indeed, the wise angler seeks out moving water while mentally ranking all his or her fishing spots.

Most people know that the moon influences tide but lack a full understanding of the purity of its cycle. Moon tides happen twice per month: when the moon is "full," large and round in the night sky; and when it is "new," full during the daytime. During both these periods, say two days either side of a new and full, is the greatest exchange of water. These periods occur roughly two weeks apart and represent extremes in available light during the nighttime. Many sources refer to these as spring tides, though they have nothing to do with the season. When we mentioned the purity of cycle earlier, we were trying to say that the moon's orbit around the earth repeats itself, taking the same amount of time, thus influencing the water with its pull in the same way. This causes tides to occur at the same time according to moon phase. For instance, a Rhode Island full moon will occur at roughly 8:15 P.M. Daylight Savings Time. That same night the tide is high at midnight on Cape Cod. Time of tide and moon phase are thus constant. The angler who knows either has to know the other. If your Rhode Island tide chart says high water is at 8:15 P.M., and you don't see anything in the sky at noon, it will be there that night: full.

Something I have chuckled over all my life is when the angler who hits the fish this Friday night right after dark can't figure out why the "hot spot" doesn't repeat itself a week later. What he has done is come back to fish nearly the opposite tide. Had he waited two weeks, however, he would have found more nearly identical conditions. A similar example lies in moon rise. I have seen many blitzes that were triggered nightly by the rise in the moon. The gang hits the fish at ten o'clock, with the moon on the eastern horizon. Next night they are back at sunset fishing their brains out until ten only to discover that the fishing doesn't materialize. Both moon and tide have moved up roughly fifty minutes in a twenty-four-hour period, and the same fish are there panting for a plug or eel at 10:50 P.M. Few of the gang are still on the beach to cash in. Moreover, when this happens in the deep night, it frequently goes unnoticed.

The above is not meant, however, to underscore fishing full- or new-moon periods exclusively. These are merely starting points in the explanation. The two remaining moon phases, the first and last quarters, enjoy just as dramatic a place. The waning moon is the last quarter, which will rise roughly between one and two in the morning, appearing at less than half size. This happens seven nights after the full moon, changes the light situation deep in the night, and generates the least amount of tidal exchange. Two weeks later, during the first quarter, the moon sets at the same time. The set or rise of the moon represents significant changes in conditions that can either spark or retard the fishing.

Reduction of tidal exchange during these quarter moons is not necessarily bad. Many spots move water too violently with moon tides to provide suitable fishing for those of us limited by how far we can cast. The more subdued currents move the fish into range in some places. Or the combination of timing between night, slack, water exchange, and available light for a given location present a set of conditions that fit that particular setting. In most cases you don't have to know tide within a few minutes. Things like tide watches or checking the chart nightly are unnecessary. If the moon was full or new two nights ago and you are fishing Rhode Island, water will top off around 10:00 P.M. Old-time calendars used to give moon phase, which automatically gave any tidewise observer the tide. I miss them.

Tide is an integral part of the timing of surfcasting. Some spots are always good, but you can't reach them unless the water is out. In places where it goes out farther, this is a greater truism. So many times we have stood in a crowd at

Race Point tonging our brains out only to have the rising water drive us away from the fish, the short guys virtually gurgling at the tail end of the blitz. Moreover, the guys who dump more line, either because of what they fish with or how well they cast, buy themselves a few extra precious moments in fish-filled waters. The subject, for all its constants and pure cycles, holds a measure of mysteries.

At East Beach, Charlestown, there is an ocean current near a place called "the Mound" that used to confound me. You could fish that beach for years, any tide, any moon phase, and have your eel come in on a straight course at any point on the shore from Fresh Pond to 200 yards this side of the breachway. Yet on the midtide drop, unaccountably, there would be a pull on the line when you fished near the Mound. Not a violent tiderip as tiderips go, but for this beach it was too distinct to either go unnoticed or unfished. I cannot say whether it was made good by my enthusiasm for this mystery tiderip or if it was one of those natural places where gamefish gather, a place only whispered between friends, but there were a few nights at midtide when it went unfished.

What astounded me about the spot is that it lacked the visible structure that we normally associate with tiderips. Most of the time your best chance at moving water is on some point of prominence that juts out into the sea, a place where normal tide flow is enhanced by a strong wind, a passage between islands, or a narrowing of an estuarine river. Anything that speeds up the water speeds up or enhances feeding opportunities for gamefish.

It may be a trifle simplistic to attribute better fishing to current alone. Often these currents are made up of warm water or yet unmixed slugs of warm water. As I said earlier, the most dramatic interchange involves backwaters, and these, being shallower and of less volume than the open sea itself, are easily warmed by the air or sun. At the Cape's Race Point, the rising tide is cold, but the evening drop is a full 10 degrees warmer. We could draw upon any number of other examples throughout New England, but one will suffice. No doubt this warm water being doled out into the sea is attractive either to bait or gamefish—little difference for our purposes. We mention all these things because it is not enough to simply know where fishing is good; to find good fishing yourself, you must know *why* it is good.

Still, the sea holds its mysteries. Any time I find stripers and blues in a place with any regularity, I find myself wondering what little ecological glitch makes it happen. Then, my tip is hauled down by a sudden take, and there is no time to think.

⇒ *Night Fishing* ⇐

For a saltwater angler who fishes the shore, specifically for stripers and bluefish, the need to fish at night is so basic that it makes me uneasy to talk about it. Still, if a lifetime of surfcasting has taught me anything, it is that people really don't do it. You could visit any number of known striper hot spots at the height of the season and be hard pressed to find someone there to talk with about the fishing.

We emphasize the basic need to fish nights, because we have tried many striper-producing areas, which were enjoying some good fishing at the time, during the day. While there have been notable occasional exceptions, most were fishless under a bright sun. Yet you could go back the next night and find the fish had returned. It isn't that these free-swimming gamefish are necessarily nocturnal, it is that the structure that surfcasters are fishing will not be used by gamefish until there is a cover of darkness. Keep in mind that these fish have survived an extremely predatory environment—the better ones for a longer time.

If you think about it, many, if not most, of our fish and mammals are nocturnal, either to practice or escape predation. I've been going hunting for forty years and have seen a fox in the woods only once in my life. Yet at night, often while moving from one fishing spot to another, I have looked upon many dozens. Even deer, which are herbivorous, are often part of some other creature's solution; these are most nocturnal in the way they function. Point here is that wild creatures utilize night cover for survival. Stripers and, to a lesser degree, bluefish are no exception. Most always the great kills of both that take place during the day in boats are a long way from the beach.

One of the most commonly accepted exceptions to the night rule is that of fall-migration fishing. Admittedly, day fishing during this period is much better than what you'll find at any other time of the year. It may be even good enough during the day to forgo night fishing. Still, whatever it is during the day, it is much better at night. I've often thought that was also because the fish are easier to fool. I risk such generalizations here because I feel strongly that you are going to catch more fish from the shore if you fish at night.

Of course the resistance to night fishing is more social than biological. It is unnatural to work daytime hours and then be fishing when you are in the habit of sleeping. Still, some of us have learned ways to get around that. If catching fish is a big part of what it is all about, these hours are mandatory. And the case can be strengthened.

Fishing the beach these days is a maze of what often seem insurmountable problems: parking, crowds, denial of access, boat traffic. Fishing in the deep night minimizes your exposure to these things.

Some of our best bathing beaches, designed to accommodate thousands of vehicles, can be utilized by the night surfcaster. I say "some," because many do not. Officials, sympathetic to the frustrations of surfcasters, are often willing to look the other way, however. Many access problems, stemming from complaints that would never stand up in court, have a way of melting away when the people nearby who do all the complaining are sound asleep. Keep in mind that we don't advocate trespassing, just exercising your rights while nobody is noticing. Of course our basic premise here—that few surfcasters are fishing at night—points up what a joy usually crowded fishing areas can be while the world sleeps. We recently fished for fluke at Point Judith's East Wall, placing our casts carefully in front of us, lest we tangle another's line. After a shore dinner in town, we went back to plug the area that night and found one other fisherman.

One of the undeniable joys of night fishing is the elbow room that I doubt this discussion will destroy. But built into the nature of night fishing is the readability of its practice. Any time you visit a hot spot in the deep night and find a crowd, you can bet they are murdering bass or blues or both.

It is very hard for me to write this because I have been night fishing so long I take for granted both the skills and difficulties involved. (It's like trying to teach walking.) I suspect that one source or resistance is that people think they can't see at night. Of course the levels of light vary both with moon phase and cloud cover, but the requirements of surf fishing don't demand that you see that well. You only have to hit the ocean with a plug or bait, and that is a pretty big target. Most fishermen have been doing what they do long enough in the daytime to be able to do it automatically at night. Most day anglers open their bail without looking down, and you can feel if the mono is fouled around the tip. But wait—there is a presupposition here that the surf is as dark as a closet. On most nights you can see when a buddy down the beach has a fish on. Breaking fish, more common at night, will show up quite well, if they are in range.

If you are not a seasoned night angler, choose your fishing areas with a little more caution, at least at first. There simply isn't anything to trip on when fishing on a sandy beach. On the other hand, if you have misgivings about the night, don't walk a long jetty or repel the Anawan Cliffs when you have easier options.

It is important to keep things simple and planned out for comfort, because the world is different at night. Most shore fishing calls for a good level of mobility and a minimal, believe it or not, amount of light. We like little, two-cell, C- or AA-size flashlights, which are rubber or plastic that you can hold in your mouth without damaging teeth when working with both hands on knots or fish takeoffs. You can get mighty thirsty, hungry, cold, or wet in the deep night. If fishing when you are supposed to, there won't be any bars or restaurants for restoring comfort. I've always kept an old pair of pants and shirt under the seat of car and beach buggy. When I started beach fishing years ago, one of the old men of the shore (Gad, he was younger than I am now!) used to scold me for not having a jug of water in my buggy, saying that it could save my life. And there is nothing like a hot coffee from a vacuum bottle to break up a slow night.

One justified fear in the deep of night concerns crime. One of our Provincetown gang was once mugged on a New York jetty, ending up with a head injury that nearly put him down for good. But, after all, he was at an inner-city location where that sort of thing is common only yards away. The example does point up that there are things you don't want to do, particularly alone. I wouldn't park a Caddy or Lincoln near the docks downtown looking for striper shadows underneath. Having a woman with you in the wrong places also invites trouble. On the other hand, people bent upon crime are not going to be at isolated spots where their victims are scarce. Moreover, because many outdoorsmen possess strong survival skills, they suffer less from fear, thus enjoying a psychological advantage over a would-be mugger. Indeed, the aggressor would be more likely to seek an easier mark than one who calmly creeps around jetties in the deep night. I've been attacked by more dogs than anything else, and being there at night wasn't a factor. Back to fishing.

Never make the mistake of thinking that because it is dark the fish can't see. No one knows for sure, but, stabbing at an explanation in human terms, fish apparently have a proximity sense that is a combination of the senses we have. Some authorities call it a "biological sonar," thought to center around the lateral line, which most fish have. This additional sense, which we either do not have, or it is less developed, permits the fish to "feel" the prey in their vicinity. I have tossed jigs

The need to use your senses is greater when fishing at night. Here, I am watching for feeding stripers in the shadow of a bridge.

into a deep channel during the lightless new moon, the current so strong that it was covered with foam while a fog so thick engulfed the seascape, closing off all light from above. In my mind no striper or blue could ever have seen it. They did. I've fished the same dark nights when an onshore wind turned the water white, blowing so hard that we couldn't cast our plugs. In desperation we heaved sinkers with streamer fly teasers that were no larger than hefty trout flies. Admittedly, we couldn't find them on the end of our own lines, but the fish did.

USING YOUR SENSES

Locating stripers is a major aspect of this surfcasting game. Doing so in the deep night calls upon the application of all your senses. True, to a large degree, the wise surfcaster can rely upon knowledge of an area, the nuances of a particular spot in terms of tide, favorable winds, and any number of considerations dealt with elsewhere in this book. But you can never know too much.

You'll need to apply all of those faculties in determining if striped bass are there. The surfcaster is not equipped with the luxuries of graph recorders, which number and place—three dimensionally—the position of gamefish. It is necessary to use the most primitive means for determining their presence. Here we will treat, according to rank order, the application of those senses to the surfcaster's best advantage toward that mission.

Finding Working Birds

Finding working birds is the most common way to determine the presence of bass. This is largely applied in day fishing, however, particularly at daybreak. When that is the case, it is usually a daylight continuation of something that has been going on all night. The birds are merely joining in at the point when they can see it. During the fall migration it is not uncommon to come upon such action at any time in daylight. There is more available bait at this season, and migrating gamefish are feeding heavier than they would at any other time of year because a higher level of energy consumption must be satisfied. This is to meet the needs of travel, then a long lean winter, followed by a spawning season that virtually depletes their store of energy.

Working birds largely comprise two species: terns and gulls. Variations and subspecies of such birds need no elaboration here. There are often subtle differences, however, in the level of interest between terns and gulls. If the bait is small, then both species will involve themselves. But when it is of the larger bait fish, that is, bunker or larger mackerel, only the gulls will become involved, because only they are able to pick up outsize bait.

In such situations fish typically will be driving bait to the surface, often into the air, and the birds will capitalize on the situation as a feeding opportunity. The notion that birds help the fish to feed as well by driving the bait downward again would be difficult to prove, but is commonly believed by surf-casting observers. It is a certainty that predators from below are helping the birds.

I have seen birds work at night, but only when there was artificial light available. This happened to my advantage in the midseventies on the Jamestown, Rhode Island, bridge. I had been walking the shadows, looking for bass, when I could see a large number of gulls collected uptide, roughly 1/10 mile east, hovering over the shadow edge. Running up the sidewalk the full distance, I cut across when I was opposite them. Once at the bridge railing, I gasped at the sight of about forty stripers moving excitedly along the shadow edge, jockeying into position to take bait there.

Tossing a bucktail jig upcurrent into the lighted portion of the sea, I saw it drift only a few feet before a 30-pound bass engulfed it. By the time I had it worn down enough for the line-gaff, hooked it, and hauled it up onto the span, the others were gone. Still, working birds had found them for me deep in the night.

Of course what working birds often tell us is that there is some serious predation going on. But there can be no guarantees that the predation is from striped bass. Indeed, just about all pelagic creatures engage in such serious bait-fish killing, from outsize mackerel to pollock, bonito, weakfish, and, most often, bluefish. But all clues have to be investigated.

Checking Out Clues

Seeing Breaks

Seeing breaks at night is possible even during the new moon phase. No question but that a fish breaking the surface will appear as a dark stain on the top. Most often the sound will attract your attention, and the dark spot—appearing as black on light black—will pinpoint its location. At this point our senses are combining, not only to determine the presence of gamefish, but to determine that point with precision. Casters who are on the stick can then lay a plug just the other side of where the bass last showed.

Finding the Bait

No gamefish is ever going to venture into shallow water for very long without the inducement of forage. While it is not always possible to determine if bait is around with any great precision, I would always draw some encouragement from locating it. One lone squid washed up on the beach can mean that tons of them have passed. A sprinkling of sand eels flushed from a boot foot grinding the sand is enough to indicate that there is good reason for stripers to be around. And a cautiously trained light on the water can cause sperling to scurry. Maybe tinker mackerel have been in the area for a week and, though you are unable to see any of them, it is a good bet that they are still around. Or it is September and 10-inch snapper blues are running.

The wise surfcaster watches for bait as well as stripers. Bass are not far from this beach.

Again, it is a case of evidence. So often when our reliable Cape Cod hot spots held nothing, we drove the beach for up to 20 miles right along the water line searching for one stick of bait, one sand eel. But when we did find that glimmering little body of striper candy, we shut down, and the bass were there.

In areas where we had not fished for some time, we often drove the beach in daylight looking for bait. Not always announced by working birds, we have seen dark clouds behind some sandbar looking like weed. In the bright sun such finds can be distinguished more easily with the help of polaroids. These allay the surface glare, allowing the eye to effectively penetrate the water's surface. Mark such caches of bait carefully, because they are excellent starting points for that night's fishing. And while we are in no position to guarantee stripers, the premise that bait means bass is a reliable one.

Sizing Slicks

Heavily feeding gamefish are going to emit digestive evidence in the form of an oil slick on the surface. Because of the schooling nature of both stripers and bluefish, there is a tendency for them both to act as one. They will attack forage at the same time, often be of similar size, and need roughly the same amount of time for their digestive processes. Thus, it appears that all the members of a school of stripers or bluefish will leave such evidence at about the same time. What helps the surfcaster is knowing what species he is dealing with.

Bluefish are tight feeders often showing up in great numbers. When the blues are leaving oil, the size of the sheen can range from as small as your living room up to as large as a 300-foot circle. But the stripers, seemingly in smaller numbers, though individually much larger, will often leave many slicks about the size of a dining table.

Reflecting upon these things, we can draw some evidence: I know which fish leave these distinctive slicks, because they were observed while taking the particular species. I have seen them most often at dawn after a frenzied night of feeding where the surfcasters who were there had taken fish all night. And, lastly, fish that are leaving slicks may be there but are less prone to the hook because their bellies are full.

In my most recent encounter involving slicks, autumn of 1989, people were leaving the beach fishless soon after daybreak. I sought to do so myself when a slick was evident in the calm surf. Having run a number of different plugs through it as it drifted seaward from an offshore wind, I was unable to draw a single taker. In desperation I tossed a live eel into the spot, questioning evidence that I was sure had merit. I couldn't get the eel back! Perhaps striped bass and bluefish are like you and me: We'll eat even when we are not hungry if it is something special.

Hearing

It is often possible to hear stripers breaking the surface when they are feeding. Admittedly, this can be difficult above the roar of a raging surf. But if it happens a hundred times within casting distance, and you hear it only once, there is clear evidence that something is in your fore. Moreover, it is more likely to happen in the wash where you are standing, because bait fish are trapped against the shore, and opportunistic stripers know it. If the surf is loud enough to obscure sound, it is more likely to happen against the beach.

Good surfcasters are detectives looking for any evidence that might point their way. I can imagine one of us, after casting for four hours to no avail, hearing one subtle "pop" and dismissing it as the imagination. This is why it is important to trust your senses. If I were too tired or discouraged to cast on, I would listen for another shred of evidence that the situation was changing. I would want to hear what I thought I heard one more time. Listen!

There is a stretch of beach south of Cape Cod's Race Point, this side of Hatches Harbor, where the surf's action pans out sand eels, and the bass there know it. Consequently, linesides will come in to feed inches from the dry shore. Many times we have walked there to flush them out, and they never do so without whirling seaward in a noisy dither to escape. Within five minutes they would be back, willing to take a slim swimming plug that had been cast down the beach.

Fishing the quieter estuaries, where there is no surf to obscure sound, it is naturally a simple matter to hear feeding. Again, is that a striped bass you have heard? Of course, in an effort to treat the subject thoroughly, intensity of sound, though not conclusive, often gives some indication of what one is dealing with. I've heard big bass in the Cape Cod Canal chasing whiting that sounded as though a mule had been tossed from the Sagamore Bridge. And I have heard subtle little plops that so sounded like schoolies, which ended up being all fish over 30 pounds. Catch them first, weigh them later.

Smell

Any time one of the beach gang says he can smell stripers, my BS meter pegs itself. More often the smelling of stripers is a figure of speech. There are situations, however, when there is a definable scent given off by the digestive activity of bass. First, there have to be enough such fish for the scent to be noticeable, the wind has to be favorable, and the person making the observation must be able to separate that of bass from that of bluefish.

It is impossible to compare this smell to that of something with which we are all familiar. Some have likened the striper smell to that of fresh melon, others thyme. It could be because we all smell things differently, but I have never been able to pick up the likeness. To me the striper smell is fishy, similar to that of bluefish, though the latter is more pungent, more fishy. The bass smell is sweeter, even more subtle.

We hasten to emphasize that smelling striped bass is not some rare skill that only a few esoteric, old-time regulars with extra-sensory powers possess. Anyone who can smell bacon frying and is astute enough to listen to his or her senses can pick it up. One does not actually smell bass, one smells digestive processes, as with the visual location of slicks. For the condition to occur in measurable amounts, of course, there must be a large enough number of schooled-up fish that have previously located bait at about the same time. Here we rely upon the same causes that created viewable slicks to produce discernible results. Moreover, it is a condition dependent upon intensity, as one can imagine that fresh-air dilution could reduce all evidence to below the threshold of detection. In lean feeding periods. like spring, you are less apt to raise the scent of a bass, because there are simply less opportunities for the fish to clobber bait in the same way they might in summer or fall. A lone striper that picks up a stray sea worm, crab, or clam isn't going to generate enough digestive activity to bring attention to itself. Thus, when we smell stripers we are detecting large-scale activity. I suppose there is always the possibility that we might confuse a school of menhaden with the aroma of stripers. But that distinction might be academic in that if we smell the bait, it would be as meaningful as scenting the gamefish themselves.

Any striper emanations are going to be carried by the winds, and there isn't a nose on the striper coast that can tell how distant the source is. It might be encouraging to have your olfactory senses titillated when standing in the suds at Race Point, but are the fish in the Race at your fore a cast away, or are they dozens of miles downwind at Billingsgate Shoals? Similarly, I have smelled bass at the old Chatham Inlet. But they could have been in any number of Monomoy rips, on either side of that island.

Even when the winds are right, scent is rarely a viable means for locating stripers. If you think about it, any school of bass that has fed enough to precipitate that level of detectable digestive activity is a poor audience for us to be offering food to. Those times that we've thought we smelled bass rarely produced any level of success that was greater than the many nights when we smelled nothing and cleaned up. Said differently, I have been into huge schools of bass hundreds of times in my lifetime without smelling a thing. A ravenously feeding school of linesides is likely to have empty digestive systems anyway.

Too much is made of smelling stripers, putting me on the fence in terms of its importance. I have also known this means of locating fish to be more a cheap way for some to raise their prestige with their fellows, a thing that is easily detected when the wind is blowing over the dunes.

I recall one year, just east of the Cape's Race Point, when we were mired in an awful doldrum, not having a fish among any of the gang for weeks. The night stripers came there had been a number of remarks about the smell, and the wind was right for it to be happening. Every regular buzzed like an excited child about the scent, so that before long it became one of those man-woman-and-child blitzes with everybody— some clad in pajamas—blitzing stripers until dawn. Personally, I think we would have had the blitz anyway, even without the smell.

My most vivid memory of smell making a serious contribution took place one night on the Outer Cape in North Truro, during an east wind. There had been a handful of us spread along the beach, maybe 20 yards apart, taking nice fish—high 30s to mid-40s—skylarking and raising hell with them as they kicked onto the plugs, some in the last wave. It had even gotten to be a game as to who could snub down a fish as it flailed in the building surf. When it began to rain, the action was so good that those of us who bothered with slickers did so between fish. The wind heightening east and the rain pelting us, things soon got pretty rough, and the fish laid off. All of the gang quit, and, chilled to the bone, we could think only of a warm, dry bunk and three fingers of hundred proof. It was time to go.

Buggy windows were fogged and the heater was on full, poor Joyce gagging from my tobacco smoke. Then, when she opened her window, the east window, a few inches to breathe, she shouted, "STOP." Only one thing could put that kind of urgency in her voice: striped bass.

Now here is a person who knew nothing of smelling striped bass, but something—call it intuitive—was telling her that smell that had drifted through that small window opening in a gale was the smell of stripers. I knew that it was the moment I stepped out of the buggy. The smell was so clear that you could have taken aging city folk who had never been to the shore and they would have told you it was fish. My poor wife was still trying to open her door into the wind when I ran down to the water. We thought that we had been into stripers before the rain! Now you didn't cast every few yards probing for them: It was a case of how many times you were hit before hooking up solid. When it is like that, one can only envision how they must be stacked out there. I suspect that a net would have needed a couple of wreckers to tow it. We were still at it when the gray dawn came, stripers sliding through the foamers in unison, apparently disappointed because they had not gotten to our plugs first. And every one was a gift of my wife's inadvertent sniff.

Digs

Now and then you will catch bass with their chins worn raw and scratchy. This is clear evidence that these fish have been rooting on the bottom. I know of three forage species, though there may be others, that will cause them to do that: sea worms, blood worms, and sand eels. I have seen stripers probing the bottom for bait in shallow water, their tails and dorsals breaking the surface, seemingly involved in a struggle to maintain their balance much in the way you and I might while standing on our heads. When they are so engaged, it is important to have your offer pass them right against the bottom, as they are not likely to see it at any other level. The largest stripers I've ever taken fly fishing were rooting the bottom, and the fly had to be retrieved with the tip in the water.

Linesides will actually dig in the bottom with their chins, making it impossible in some places to find evidence of this digging. I must emphasize, however, that dig holes can only be found under ideal conditions, which, the best I can define, would be a very fine sand bottom. I don't think this is the most important aspect of locating stripers, but I have never known of it being reported before, and it serves to remind us how little is known about our quarry. We first discovered these striper digs on Outer Cape Cod in the Truro/Wellfleet area, where we had been in the habit of catching large stripers from 30 to 50 pounds.

Here the many finger bars running perpendicular to the beach can be waded at low tide for a cast into deep water. One night I noticed a number of bunny holes that I could feel with my feet; these were only a few inches deep, roughly the size of a grapefruit. Yet where the tide had gone out fully, there was no evidence of the holes, because the wave action in the shallows apparently erased them. Thus, any time that there was evidence of these marine woodchucks, it had to be fresh: the last tide. Subsequently, we learned that fishing was usually good when the holes were in evidence. And we also found that many of our fish had slight abrasions on their chins on nights when we found the holes. From then on we waded deep at any stage of tide, feeling for the "tracks" of stripers.

I have since noticed, interestingly, that my own early casts are rarely made with any true faith in the fishing. It is more a case of needing something to do while assessing the surf around me. The astute surfcaster should be watching, listening, sniffing, and feeling for any evidence that linesides are about; they often tell those of us who just know how to know that they are there.

KNOWING THE SHADOWS

There is a condition that occurs around well-lighted bridges and piers that appeals to many gamefish, particularly stripers. This is the shadow that develops from a combination of the structure itself and the light above it. Within that shadow gamefish will lurk, waiting for a chance to grab some of the bait that is attracted to the light.

Certainly, our coastline is dotted with enough bridges and docks to provide more than you'll ever need in fishing spots. Dealing with them is where the problems are. First, you have to know what to look for and where to look. All of the situations will have a shadow line that is out from the dock or bridge a few yards. The lighted portion is outside that shadow. You have to focus your vision on the inside edge of the shadow where the gamefish will usually be lying still. We say "gamefish" because blues and weakfish will do this, but stripers—more likely the bigger ones—seem to prefer feeding this way above all others. When you see one it will appear as a darker black silhouette on a black background. Just how apparent the outline is depends upon how deep the fish is lying. Of course it is important that, while you are moving around, your own shadow is not being projected upon the water in a

Cupping his eyes, this angler is watching for bait or stripers lurking in the bridge shadows below.

way that precedes your own movements. These fish are spooky and can be sent hell-west by any discernible movement from above.

If there is any current, and on bridges there usually is, foragers will be facing it. Sometimes a fish will take up a line in front of a piling or slightly to the side of it to take advantage of the break in current. Thus, it is not enough to just eyeball the inside of a shadow; you have to stop and try to look way under at the bridge or dock structure itself. This is more important on bridges where the water is moving at a height in tide change.

Competent bridge fishermen will walk a shadow edge looking for fish first. If they can't find any, then they will work the little eddies or breaks in current blindly, in the hope that there is a fish holding that they were unable to see. Naturally, once that has been ruled out, you can go into a system of working water, a few feet between each cast, where your offer is allowed to sink deep, covering water where your eyes have been unable to penetrate. Of course, things are changing all the time, influenced by tide and traffic, and the shadow you walked an hour ago could have any number of fish showing after you've worked an area the hard way. Very often, while making deep passes because I hadn't seen anything, I have noticed a big striper swimming at an angle along the edge of a shadow. They take this angular position so that they can advance while still looking upcurrent for something to grab. Their movement at times can be so fast that it is all you can do to keep up with them, while avoiding spooking them with your shadow. Even when you pass one enough to make a cast, if he doesn't see it, by the time you've reeled in and opened the clutch he is gone and you have to make another run to get ahead.

Such experiences can be pretty frustrating, not only because of the work they take and the demands of a well-placed cast, but because these fish don't always like what you are throwing at them. Wild stripers are just like wild trout or anything else in that they don't always take.

I've seen a number of methods used in bridge and pier fishing: bucktail jigs (with or without squid strips), the long-billed Rebel, live eels, live pogies, or herring in season. But the most effective one, where current is passing through the shadows, is the bucktail jig: This is a small, easy-to-cast lure that offers the best sinking options while providing enough strength to stand up to the unusually heavy fighting forces with which you'll be confronted. Unlike a beach, where a fish can be given its head for a run, fish caught on the edges of bridges and docks are going to take off with the current. This means that there are always going to be barnacle-encrusted obstacles that a heavy fish could wrap a line around. It is a case of big-game stand-up control that goes beyond most widely used casting equipment, because with any luck we are talking 40-pound stripers here.

If you are comfortable with it, conventional tackle is best, and the mono shouldn't be any lighter than 30; because distance isn't a factor, you can spool up 30-pound—no more than that—on a heavy spinning reel. Most of the time when you are into a good fish, it will go down current under the bridge, and if it moves to either side making headway, you are at risk of having your line contact a support. For this reason you have to try to hold all hookups right on the spot, which can be a jarring experience for angler and tackle alike.

The very nature of such places provides some pretty nasty landing challenges. I cannot think of one dock or bridge where beaching a fish is possible after hooking it under these conditions. Tide and structure depending, reaching down from a dock with a long-handled gaff calls for some good shooting on a fish that is spent enough for an easy shot with the iron. If you are alone, everything has to be carried to a greater degree of expertise. If you are fishing from a very long bridge where you'll be hooking fish ¼ mile or more from land, it is not as easy as you think to walk a big bass to shore. Every piling that you walk it past poses a risk, admittedly declining as the fish is sapped of energy. The real killer, however, is what towing a big fish does to your back. It is our physiological nature to be able to withstand forces on our backs from the front, not from the side. It seems we have no muscles developed that can take punishment from side forces. I once walked a 37-pounder to shore that I hooked maybe ³⁄₁₀ mile out, and I was in agony by the time we had the thing on the beach. I had no history of back problems, and I was hurting for a few days. I've seen buddies take turns; then there are *two* sore backs.

Anybody who is going into bridge fishing seriously (try it first) needs a bridge gaff. This is a grappling hook that would fit in a circle of say 8 inches; it comprises four very sharp prongs that are welded together with an eyebolt at the top much in the style of a giant treble hook. The rope attached should be ¼ inch. There are thinner nylon lines that are strong enough, but these tend to dig into the hands. Exactly 13 inches above the points, a bronze snap is positioned, which permits you to clip the "line gaff" on when the fish is spent below you.

We all carry our gaffs in a shoulder bag, and once we are ready to use it, clip it to the line and lower it until it stops on the fish's head. You have to lift it gently, hoping that it doesn't spin and foul on the line. Once the fish is impaled, you must open the clutch or bail on your reel so that if it falls off while coming up, the line won't be broken. We had a guy reeling line on the way up once, and he lost his rod when the big bass fell off. Another thing to remember about the physical demands of hauling a big fish, say more than 40 pounds, is that it can do some nasty things to your shoulder muscles. (My best this way is 46, but I'm not getting any younger.) Lastly, don't throw the gaff rope out into the road while hauling the fish up.

Most of the fish that are going to be hunting these kinds of shadows won't move in until things quiet down. Docks with heavy boat traffic in summer shouldn't be approached until late in the night. Bridges suffering from gridlock or heavy summer traffic are bothersome to fishing and seem to keep fish away from the shadows. Late in the night or early morning before dawn, with only an occasional passing vehicle, the fish are not bothered.

Keep in mind that this situation is dependent upon darkness. Moonlit nights will wash out a shadow, making it impossible for an angler to see fish and no doubt allay any effort gamefish might put into a fuzzy shadow.

Of the two I prefer the bridges, the longer ones that provide a longer shadow to hunt. There is something especially challenging in being high above the water and bracing yourself against the force and violent thrashing that suddenly comes to a jig when moments before it was drifting harmlessly in the current. Then, in spite of all efforts to prevent a single yard of mono from leaving the spool, you are cranking more yards than you cast, the creosote of a bridge's underside staining your hands, and you get the feeling of how close you came to big trouble.

Beach Shadows

Our first experience with the influence of shadows came long before we ever fished the bridges. It was another of those delightful accidents that you can come upon while fishing the beach that ends up serving you a measure of polished surf-casting.

It was in the early seventies when we first started fishing Race Point on Cape Cod. Few people then knew how good the Race was for surfcasting. For us it was a family secret, and we parked at a place called the Second Rip, which later became known as Race City. When the tide was right, we would drive east late at night, then take the back trail west to Race Light where a gaggle of buggies was always parked in a line. There was a shorter way, but the direct route would have tipped off too many people as to our destination. The vehicles there were the big walk-in types, occupied by boat fishermen who fished by day and could be counted upon to be sound asleep at night. Far be it for us to wake them.

Those rigs were parked in so tight, and the angle between them and Race Light was so long, that they cast a black shadow upon the surf when the water level was about mid-tide. Yet there was always an open spot, arbitrarily spaced, which permitted the light through, illuminating the surf. Of course the Race usually could be counted upon to provide more than a measure of stripers and blues, and it had been our habit to disperse ourselves around that point, casting Rebels into the falling currents from Cape Cod Bay. The night we discovered the influence of shadows there, however, most of us were not catching any bass. But our twins, Susan and Sandra, were sliding linesides back to the truck with uncanny regularity. I was getting suspicious that they might be onto something unusual when I noticed a little hostility between them. Apparently one of them had lingered at the other's shadow edge, which was a distinct turf violation in her mind. After a stern diatribe on politeness and sportsmanship, I permitted Susan to teach me the shadow ropes.

The sea was in full drop, left to right, so that when she cast her plug straight out from the beach it swung a hard right under tension into the lighted spot. Positioned so that the plug was at about 45 degrees from her, it would swing into the shadow of the next big buggy, where the bass were lined up and panting. She claimed that there were virtually no hits in the lighted portion of the surf, and upon demonstration she hooked a 20-pounder on her second cast. The whole thing was uncanny!

Naturally, after that first night, the arrangement of the buggies became a point of conjecture and interest with us all. And we were subsequently to learn that lights and shadows contained their own body of knowledge. First of all, nearly all hits came at the precise moment when the beam of Race Light illuminated the surf. Then, and it has changed since, it took thirteen seconds for a rotation of the light. During those thirteen seconds the sea was dark, uninfluenced by the brightness and the resultant shadows. Of course we did catch some stripers outside of shadow edges and outside the influence of what we speak here. But there was another phenomenon not at all uncommon to the place: fog.

Fog is but millions of droplets of water suspended in the air. What is Cape Cod but a place shrouded in fog? And what is

Race Light but one of the foggiest spots on Cape Cod? Nights when the Race was enveloped in the stuff, and there were many, these droplets would dutifully serve to bounce the light all over the seascape for so long that one cycle of the light virtually ran into another, so that the influence of the light was nearly constant. I don't think the improved shadow conditions brought more fish into our surf, but it did heighten the efficiency with which we fished. Instead of running the risk of having your plug go through the shadow edge at a time when the lights were out, the chances increased that it would pass the magic point in the time lapse of suitable striking—when droplets were bouncing those candle powers all over the shore. Use of the shadows worked, and it put a lot of fish on the beach.

We dwell upon this, not because it is so important to surfcasting, but because it is a subject that I believe has never received much if any treatment by other surfcasting writers. Before going on I will allude to one more shadow example, not because it is paramount to your education on the high surf, but because it is truly unusual.

A few years later, our twin girls in high school by then, we located a serious concentration of big bass in Truro on Cape Cod. For a number of consecutive nights, we had caught large numbers of fish in the 30- to high-40s range at corners where sandbars, running perpendicular to the beach, met the shore. But once the tide started in, these hot spots became increasingly difficult to locate with any degree of accuracy, and the infusion of new water had the effect of dispersing the stripers. I cursed the rise for driving us out of such good fishing. At that stage of tide it became necessary to fish the beach arbitrarily, farming a lot more water for what fish were available. Dropping Joyce first, I would spread the twins 1/10 mile apart, leave about the same distance, then shut the buggy down, leaving it behind for Joyce to pick up everybody with. In this way we could cover a mile of beach in a relatively short time. And we had covered a couple of miles in this way to no avail when our two little *darlings* signaled that they had fish on.

Spinning the rig around in a tight circle against the dunes without headlights, Joyce and I went to their rescue, taking up casting stations on either side, yet not so close as to interfere with their fighting the fish. But for us there was nothing. The more linesides that they hooked, the closer we ventured, but our failure to shoulder right in on them made it seem as though either we were cursed or they were charmed—yet our plugs and teaser rigs were identical!

Not that they would ever withhold information from us, but I knew that they preferred to have their old father idle, serving their every need than have him busily engaged in fishing of his own. Their mother was a different story. After calling her over, they urged her to cast at a point in their fore, permitting the plug to drift nor'west to a dark patch of water where it was a certainty that a cow could take the thing down as though it were the last edible thing in the Atlantic. And that dark patch of sea was the shadow of a high dune that towered behind us, blocking out the light from a gibbous moon. The entire shore was bathed in silvery moonlight, but at that particular spot, one prominent dune reached into the sky, and the angle was perfect for the projection of a sizable-enough shadow. Moreover, moon phase and tide being interrelated, the condition occurs every moon, we later learned (though we should have known). That water flowed into the shadow, instead of out of it, was simply a toss of a coin in our favor.

For many years after I searched the beach for other places where this phenomenon might repeat itself, always to no avail. Such a condition calls for a beach that faces the northeast with a dune high enough to block out the moonlight. Had I been lucky enough to find such a place, it would only have done what it had to do a few nights each month.

LIGHT AT NIGHT

The utilization of shadows is rare when unnatural situations of light contribute to the fishing. For the most part the light involved is stationary (or predictable) enough so that it does not spook gamefish from the surf. But it would be unwise for any surfcaster to forget that the quarry are wild animals and that millions of years of natural selection have bred a wariness into them. Only those with the greatest measure of cautiousness lived long enough to pass it on. All wildlife, of course, have made adaptations to the presence of man. No doubt this is why marine gamefish do not fear well-lighted bridges and lighthouses on our coastal promontories. Still, there are certain assumptions that would be in our best interest if we are to successfully approach these wild creatures in order to better fish for them.

Life in the sea is one of constant predation, where everything in it is feeding upon another life form. These creatures learn quickly that they too are another creature's solution. As a result the slightest movement or change in their environment terrorizes them into an escape mode. Keep in mind that these fish so fear attack both from above and from the land that they only rarely venture into shallow water and only when there is adequate promise of a suitable food return. The relatively shallow surf represents a dangerous and hostile environment that gamefish generally will only chance under the cover of darkness. Those rare occasions when fish feed in close in daylight occur when there are either ample foraging opportunities in the form of acres of bait or when hunger is increased by the energy consumed in migration. It is the intensity of the lure that brings them into the face of danger.

Motion, I am sure, is what triggers fear in these brief surf visitors, but they are unable to discern motion when their environment is beside ours. Even at night there is too much light above the sea. Moreover, the angle to the horizon between surf anglers and surf fish makes their viewing of us nearly impossible: only slightly, if at all, under the most extreme conditions. It might be a mistake to try to evaluate the senses of gamefish in human terms, however, though, admittedly, it is all that we have. I would prefer to view a fish's perception of our presence as a combination of its perceived motion and vibration: a proximity sense. Any messages that we send threaten the disclosure of our presence. My memory yields an excellent example.

For many years we fished the shore between Race Light and Hatches Harbor on nights when the bass were feeding so close to the beach that they could have been taken with a frog spear. The limit to just how close to shore was determined as that amount of water needed to cover a striper's back—1½ feet and a depth of 8 inches for a school fish. If we walked the shore carelessly without fishing it first, the bass would flush from the shallows a few feet ahead of us with a noisy swirl. Our fatal error was that they could be taken a cast out from the beach; or, if we waited for ten minutes, very near to where they had been. Knowing this proved to be most productive for us, especially when large numbers of fish were doing it. From time to time, however, there would either be no fish, because there was no bait to draw them, or so few that walking the shore was inefficient. I recall one period when we drove our buggy along the water line, without headlights, the wheels a foot from the water, until we flushed a bass that left with a noisy surface pop. Then we would shut down and cast and nearly always took one lone bass. What drove him from the shallows, frightening him enough to betray his presence? Was it the motion of the buggy? Might it have been the vibrations of the vehicle, crushing of the sand?

Years ago, in Charlestown, Rhode Island, when buggies were permitted to drive the front beach year long, the boys there theorized that the lumbering of the buggies drove the fish out of the surf. They believed this because they could take bass all week long until Friday night when there was a continuous stream of weekend vehicles lumbering down the beach. Saturday night the fishing was always a little better because of the reduced traffic. Of course it may not have been vibrations, but rather the headlights of the vehicles on the water. Moreover, never forget that fishermen's perceptions of nights when they are not there are bound to be overblown. If that is the case, then we may inadvertently be addressing human behavior rather than that of striped bass. Nevertheless, I was going to say that motor vehicle headlights have to be the ultimate transgression upon the natural environment, especially if they are moving.

Time after time, when the fishing was good, someone has pulled up with their buggy blasting lights upon the water, putting an end to what we had. I will admit, however, that the good fishing usually resumed within a few minutes. Again, these are wild animals, and they are not going to stay in an area where their well-being is threatened. What the vehicle headlights seem to do is drive fish out for a few minutes, and their return depends upon the intensity of their interest in what brought them there in the first place. Both remain unknown quantities in this admittedly most speculative discussion.

Similar results can be expected with the use of lanterns on the beach. Many surfcasters are in the habit of setting up such things in order to improve their view of baited lines and to better see what they are doing while working with the rods. Of course it is impossible to move around such a lantern without casting eerie shadows upon the surf, generating motion that I believe is counter to keeping catchable fish in the surf. Proponents of the use of lights will argue that light lures bait into the surf. Lights may not drive bait out, but I have seen no evidence that they lure bait in. Careless use of mining lights, usually worn around the neck, no doubt yield similar results. My premise here is simply that light is unnatural and that it generates motion, which is bound to frighten something that is itself predatory.

The subject of lights on the surf is highly controversial. Most surfcasters object to them. There is of course a stubborn minority who feel that they have a right to use them as they see fit, so the dispute rages. I say it that way because I can think of no better way to alienate yourself from your fishing friends than by illuminating the better part of a place where everybody knows that the fishing is usually good. It is important here to understand that an improved level of cooperation between anglers is good for everybody. I have known some surfcasters who never believed that their lights hurt the fishing. Still they refrained from using them when others were around, because they viewed it as a case of good interpersonal politics.

Effective eye management is important to surfcasters. Specialists all say that excessive sunlight can hinder your night vision; the best protection from that is sunglasses, preferably polaroids, which can double for use in seeing through the surface glare of the daylight surf. Night exposure to bright lights, which temporarily dilates the pupils, hinders your night vision. In this case intensity has a direct influence upon the degree of impairment. Even the softest, most discreet lights hurt your ability to see after the light is out. Conversely, the less a light is used, within limits, the less it is needed.

MAKING THE MOST OF DAYBREAK

If forty years of hunting and fishing have taught me anything, it is that daybreak is one hour of the day you don't want to miss. When I was a small boy, Papa used to wake my brother and me for the field amid the smell of frying bacon, saying, "Let's go, boys. Either you get up now or you can stay in bed the rest of the day." He never had to tell us twice.

Since then I've come to love fishing the beach, and, along with that love, I've also developed an abiding respect for that magical time when a new day is sagging in the east. The reason you are more likely to take more fish per hour at this time apparently ties in with the fact that gamefish have had all night to move into the shallows. And they know, with the brightening, that they will soon have to move out. They take with such abandon that it seems as though they are trying to capitalize on their last feeding opportunity. I've always believed this to be true of all species—fresh and salt—but nowhere is it more evident than while fishing the shore, particularly for bluefish. Even if you've been taking fish all night, you won't be able to help but notice a heightening of activity

This fine bass lingered well into the daylight.

at the crack of dawn. Moreover, if the blues are around but haven't been taking in the dark, it is nearly certain they will make a pass along the beach before heading out to deep water to sulk for the day. Researchers are certain that blues are triggered into a feeding frenzy at dawn to a greater degree than most other marine species. Years ago some marine lab in New Jersey played games with bluefish in a tank by slowly turning up the lights while the water was filled with bait. They found that the blues would clean up the tank as soon as the light improved.

Of course that is not to say that blues alone exhibit this kind of behavior when triggered by sunrise. I'm convinced that stripers run a close second to them in exhibiting the trait. Also, stripers are more vulnerable to delay if feeding opportunities are holding up. Naturally, other factors come into play. An overcast sky can both delay and lengthen the dawn. Any of our surf gamefish will linger under the cover of rough water for a longer time; and I think them less spooky if deep water, where relative safety is close at hand, isn't too much of a swim. Keep in mind that wild, predatory fish are not likely to allow themselves to become victims of some other creature. It is a system, I'm sure, within which they function.

Granted, for the surfcaster, the beach is a nighttime proposition, but there is a brief period when enough light is available to actually look for fish. Anybody equipped with a buggy would do well to run the beach at this time. Of course there will be times when bass or blues will be blowing up the water on bait. Just seeing a pod of forage also can be signal enough to try the spot as fish will often lie in the vicinity. Sometimes, and this happens just often enough for mention here, you'll see the dorsal of a striper lying in the shallows; and sometimes, again just often enough, he will take.

If this magical time has a failing, it is that it is too short. When used to its fullest advantage, we talk forty-five minutes, unless rough water, overcast, or migration influences add a little time. But if you stick with the realities of long-term figures, most days don't provide any of those factors. For that reason it is imperative that any angler planning to fish the dawn be in the water while it is still full dark. My experience has been that far too many early-morning surfcasters wait until full light to start fishing or can't get out of bed early enough to start on time. Many instances when we picked bass all night, there would be a wild flurry just as the east was brightening, but it would end once you could see. Then the dawn patrol, buggies driving the beach, would come down, oblivious to the fishing we had had. Earlier, when I mentioned driving the beach at dawn, I was talking about driving *off.*

Personally, the dawn fishing is far too short for me. If I am going to stretch it out, I do so at the dark end, when chances of locating taking fish are far greater. Anyone fishing too early at 4:00 A.M. is way ahead of the person exercising his or her casting arm at 6:00 A.M. under a bright sun. We cling to the surfcaster's premise that ours is largely a night game. It may be a small advantage that wouldn't be strong enough to stand by itself, but the late end of the night goes largely unfished. Hot spots like the breachways in Rhode Island or the Cape's Race Point, to name only a few, often have impossible crowds, with either a line of casters or little room to cast. Evenings, particularly Fridays, everybody is panting to fish, but that can fade fast when we take into account that they have worked all day, driven to the shore, and have had to spend the night on the beach. Anybody that makes it that far is going to be part of a very small crowd if any. Nor is it only a case of having enough room to fish. When yours is the only plug or eel in the surf, it simply has a better chance of being taken. I'm convinced that excessive beach activity drives fish out of the surf, what with the rumble of vehicles being felt in the sand and magnified in the water together with headlights on the sea that can send stripers and blues hell west. It is never like that in the deep night. That is why there is something to be said for being out of step.

Timing is the heart of fishing the early-morning beach. I always look up "legal" sunrise in the local paper's almanac and actually write it down. The magical time to be fishing is about forty minutes before that, when there is a false-dawn dull glow in the east that is so slight you question if it is there. Working the time backward, I subtract the time I need to get there.

Certainly any methods that have been productive in the deep night should continually be employed while the light is changing. There is nothing wrong with using an eel or swimming plug just because you can see. Unaccountably, there seems to be some widely held dictum that methods should change with daylight; don't change what has been working. On the other hand, if things are dead there is nothing to be lost by bending a splashy popper, both to increase casting range and to attract attention.

Assuredly it is the best hour of the day to be fishing, though it lacks guarantees. I tend to forget the empty mornings, while those that have paid off vie in my memory as examples. Take the time I pulled up to a hot spot, buggies everywhere, spiked rods far from the water, left behind by a falling tide. Surfmen were all nodding and leaning, oblivious to the brightness in the east and to bait that sprinkled against the shore. Any other night I might have been among them— you know we all miss our share of blitzes, all tire and fault in the same way. But this particular morning I was on time, able to cast those few brief minutes when bass and blues raided the beach before daylight moved them out.

⇐ *Adversity in the Surf* ⇒

When you look at the list of things that can ruin a surfcaster's trip, it is a wonder that there can be any fishing at all. The sport is replete with adversities with which the beach angler must learn to cope. Crowds, boat traffic, bright moonlight, heavy seas, and fire in the water. Then, having notably dealt with all of these, we take a bad step, or misjudge the surf, and soak ourselves from head to toe.

CROWDS

Face it, it is an overpopulated world. Time after time you will make solid plans based upon tide, your available time, the season, and everything that you've learned about surfcasting. Then, to your dismay, there will be so many other anglers there that you may as well head for home. All fishing demands a measure of solitude; yet I have often thought that if I could open a hot dog stand at some of the Striper Coast hot spots, I could earn enough money to finance a trip to Australia, where perhaps I might be able to surfcast alone. But it doesn't have to be that way.

Surfcasting is a tough game; any number of things can count you out.

The average person is a wimp, and many surfcasters are no exception. If we may generalize, most people are not able to stay awake late into the night, or stand the cold, or even anticipate the beginning and end of a surfcasting season. Some fear the dark, others a heavy surf. Fact is that the behavior of most people is quite predictable. For instance, you can be certain that most fishermen—boaters or surfcasters—will be out on Friday night and that they will tire quickly from a day of work and the travel they put in getting to the beach. They are more likely to fish effectively on Saturday night, because they have had a day to rest and will have another to recover. One of the most productive weekend times to be fishing, if you can arrange it with your own schedule, is Sunday night. Naturally, holiday weekends end up multiplying the angling participation geometrically.

Your challenge is to place yourself out of step with the mob of people rushing to summer homes, marinas, lodging, and beaches. You know that the highways are going to be on the edge of gridlock at times, yet only a few hours into the night, interstates are empty. Even the most classic striper hot spots will be thinning by midnight—an excellent time for you to *begin* fishing. Depending on the season, you can enjoy four to six hours of relative solitude until the dawn fishing crowd shows up, which is a far smaller group than those at sunset.

It took me a long time to learn to control my enthusiasm on Friday afternoons. For years I ran to the shore after work like everybody else until I learned to unplug the telephone, strip down, and climb under the covers at home after work. Three or four hours of sleep is a great way to unwind from a day's work, letting the race begin without you. Then, between a huge meal and drive to the shore, the evening hours melt away, putting me on the beach at about the time when others are either nodding in their vehicles or passing us on the highway headed the other way. Nobody can take what people do to themselves every Friday in the name of surf fishing.

I have witnessed the failures of others to cope with this curse all my life. All too often they have not even fished enough to establish how good or bad the fishing was. The most classic example that tempts me here is the Columbus Day weekend I spent in Charlestown, Rhode Island. Back then I belonged to a fishing club that enjoyed a friendly dispute over where the best striper fishing was—there or on the Cape. A bunch of the gang, who had tired of the long ride to the Cape, decided to come to Charlestown in order to put the disagreement to rest for all time. I was asleep in my camper at the time that they came, roughly ten of them, but our children saw them pass on the beach. After a slow, two-coffee wake up, I started eeling the beach with my brother Norman well before midnight. At that time, I saw the lights on in only one buggy, and he was going to bed. From that time on we never saw another surfcaster.

After roughly an hour of fishing, my brother landed a fish of 35 pounds, then I caught one a little smaller. A slow pick ensued, and between us we landed eleven linesides from 23 to 45 pounds. It was so quiet during the hours we fished that we hadn't even bothered to put the fish away. Then, as the first glow to the east announced the end of night, we stowed the bass, brewed coffee, and stood around outside. The number of vehicles that came down the beach that autumn morning astounded us. Every imaginable model and year of four-wheel-drive passed us as though the devil himself was on its tail, and they came back in the other direction within minutes. Those we spoke to complained bitterly of a poor migration that year or of how fishing was in serious decline. They had driven a 4-mile stretch of striper beach and seen nothing. (The gang from the club hadn't even bothered to get out of bed.)

One of the malcontents—without even inquiring how we had done, or whether we had even fished—told me later that day that I could "keep Rhode Island." I truly wish that it were mine to keep.

MOONLIGHT

Bright moonlight is another of those natural things that can ruin you. If striped bass fear the day, then they certainly suffer from a measure of distrust for nights bright enough to read a watch. Two things can be used to ameliorate this condition: a cloud cover, which includes fog; and a running surf. Both of these provide enough cover for stripers to chance the shallows of the shore. When either of these occur, the fishing may in fact be better, because the linesides are enjoying conditions that they have not had for a few nights. You might take those conditions into account when deciding which nights are best to expend your resources.

ROUGH WATER

There is a fine line in choosing the intensity of a running sea. Big water can create marvelous surfcasting, particularly if it is wind-whipped. On the other hand, a whole gale can turn the surf into a mire of suspended sand and weed that makes fishing impossible. No more than you and I would enjoying being out in a sandstorm, the gamefish will be driven out of the surf by the silt, far from attracted to it.

The second thing that can bring up the surf is a hurricane, and you don't want ever to be at the shore during one. Too many of us forget how powerful and devastating such tempests can be. The 1938 hurricane, which occurred when I was two, killed people who were ½ mile from the beach. Its tidal wave left Rhode Island State Police stranded on telephone poles clinging to their lives. Many of us believe that it can happen again. Of course rare as such extreme situations might be, there have since been close to one hundred storms that passed close enough to the shore to ruin fishing. Never discount a hurricane that is passing east of Bermuda as being too far away to affect your fishing. Indeed, such storms will kick up a rolling surf for many hundreds of miles, their foamers breaking ¼ mile off the beach, rolling white the rest of the way until they batter the sand.

There is a danger in these generalized discussions. The choice of whether to fish a particular location when the wind blows, or when the forces of storms exert themselves, is highly dependent upon the location. Which way a beach faces, the currents that pass it, and the intensity all figure in on the decision. Easterly facing beaches are ruined by nor'easters as well as passing hurricanes. A strong sou'west can help Rhody fishing within limits. Yet the same wind, which is down your throat at Race Point, Cape Cod, could never blow hard enough there to foul the surf, because it is constantly swept by currents of clean water from way offshore.

These are just some of the complexities of interrelating conditions with particular locations. It is thus impossible to plan with the certainty we would like for a bait-laden first wave that causes a plug to drum from the vibrations of falling water, where winds complement our casts and seas are always clean.

Even then, if you are going to trip and soak yourself to the skin in a hostile sea, it can end as a night you would prefer to forget. (Forgetting bad nights is one of those inexorable qualities of fishing writers, from which I am not exempt.) This, dear reader, is why I am so good at telling stories of good fishing and totally incapable of recalling the bad. I've actually had a few less bad nights, because I wouldn't dream of fishing without a pair of old trousers and wool shirt mildewing under the seat of my vehicle until that time of need.

FIRE

By definition "fire" is actually swarms of phosphorescent microorganisms, called dinoflaggellates by scientists, which can cause anything that tips them to glow in the surf. There are hundreds of species of phosphorescent plankton in the oceans of the world.

On dark nights fire is the saltwater fisherman's curse when it glows in the breaking waves. Or every slight motion in your lure is magnified and accented as it tips the glowing plankton. Worse, your line glows right to the plug, making it all too evident that what you are fishing is attached to something. It is unnatural, it looks wrong, the fish see it, we see it, and I *hate* it!

Why wouldn't any surfcaster dislike the "fire?" These bioluminescent microorganisms can make a plug look the size of a canoe paddle and do nothing to help the fishing. And don't get the feeling that fire is unusual, because during the warmer months you can have it every night, getting a rest from the stuff only on bright nights when the moon gives off so much light that it "appears" to be gone.

We struggle to find them, but there are a few good things to be said. You surely know that the fish are around when an average-size striper follows your plug in, looming big like a sea monster—a canoe following the canoe paddle. The trouble is that all you are getting is a follow. You know where the fish are when glowing zings turn to take bait in the fire. And I'm convinced that I can tell the bass from the bluefish by the way they move in the fire. The blues have a faster scoot when feeding in the surf and seem to turn up slightly less fire with their movement. Outsize stripers are downright frightening, and a pip-squeak 20-incher can look awfully big. Even the bait can turn up enough fire to highlight themselves. When the bait fish panic, all dashing together, you can bet that you will see the illuminated whoosh of a striper or blue lunging at them within seconds. That is all I have to say that is good about the fire.

How then do those who want to catch fish deal with this sparkling marine nuisance? The less fire that we turn up, the more subtle and effective our presentation. This means staying on the lighter side when choosing lines. Conventional-reel anglers should avoid braided line. Scale down the size of all lures and baits by using the smallest plugs possible. For instance, if you like the Rebel, Red-fin, Rapala genre of swimmers, opt for the 5-inch models over the 7. Rigged-eel fishermen should use smaller baits. If you think about it, there are a number of things that we customarily have ahead of plugs that ought to be dropped because they turn up too much fire. Wire leaders look like a broom handle and ought to be removed in favor of the risk of having your line cut by bluefish. Such wire leaders also have a barrel at one end and a snap at the other, which is just more junk that will have an exaggerated appearance. The cutoff risk—if blues happen to be around—isn't that great, because they tend to bite from the rear. Even snap-swivels are an encumbrance to the subtle effect that we are trying to achieve; tie direct. Naturally, with the above in mind, teasers or droppers would be counterproductive. Both the teaser itself and the swivel it comes off of will collectively turn up as much glow as the main item that you're casting.

With all these microscopic animals drifting passively in the sea, the idea is to bump and upset as few as possible. Books say that their density can be as many as five hundred to the inch. For that reason this kind of fishing succeeds with less casts by leaving the plug out there and either minimizing its movement or slowing the retrieve just past a tight line. For one thing existing current will usually give you all the plug motion you need, and you can gain a fish's attention more easily with fire because it so highlights the presence of the plug. I'm convinced that bait fish employ the same evasive maneuver because I have often found sperling and sand eels resting in the surface tension immobile—at least until something came after them. We have taken many stripers and blues with swimmers dead-resting on the top.

Earlier we touched upon the fact that fire's visible intensity is inversely proportional to light. Depending upon the intensity of a plankton bloom, a full or quarter moon will usually allay the condition. The wise surfcaster keeps moon phase in mind, however, realizing that you are either going to lose your light with moonset or gain it at the rise in the moon. During the first quarter, you should be thinking of peeling off extra terminal tackle in anticipation of the moon going down sometime during the night and planning upon fishing any way you would like during the last quarter, when the moon rises during the night. Moreover, if fire is ruining the fishing at that time, it is liable to get mighty good once the moon comes up. Sometimes you can find unnatural light to put the fire out for you. At the Cape's Race and Highland Lights, the seascape around these lighthouses is so bathed in light for a few moments each revolution that the condition is mitigated drastically. Same holds true for downtown seawalls that are usually well lighted. And bridges nearly always have enough streetlights glowing over the water to dim the fire. While these lights are unnatural, they are constant and do more to lure gamefish than to keep them away.

It may be a little simplistic to even imply that the only consideration we surfcasters have to worry about is fire. With or without the stuff, other variables have to be taken into account. For instance, if there are many fish competing, our errors in turning up these microorganisms are less likely to be an influence; and if feeding has been lean, the fire will matter less. Indeed, for all the nights ruined, there have been many when we were panting at the buggy from the blitz we had. Not because of fire, but in spite of it.

The bioluminescence has generated more than its share of both folklore and fear. Time was, say twenty-five years ago, when we believed that the stuff was pollution. Fact is that it can be found in both the most polluted and clean waters of New England. We do not know, however, if water quality is a factor with some of the many species or no consideration at all with any of them. Also, in those days, as strapping young men who feared nothing, we never wanted to admit how spooky the stuff made us feel. One time at Mill Gut (Colt Drive, Bristol, Rhode Island) my brother, Norman, who was way out on the mussel beds at full tide, just started running for no apparent reason. This is not easy when the water is 2 inches from the top of your waders. When confronted later about his apparently irrational behavior, poor Norm said that he'd thought he saw something coming at him.

Another old surf buddy used to watch to farm the whole beach, saying that if we spread out, our collective chance of finding the bass was greater. Yet nights when the *Pyrodinium* were bumping each other from horizon to high water, he would fish under my casting arm. I once told him that if he was going to spend the night with me the least he could do was take me out to dinner. We had one guy on the Cape, muscles rippling under his Marine Corps tattoo, who would suit up with waders and foul-weather gear on a flat night, yet fish ankle deep when the waves of sparkling fireworks were about. I would have asked him if his waders leaked, but a slight-statured Frenchman was not a thing he feared.

SAFETY HAZARDS

Fishing the beach is fraught with hazards. A large comber is capable of hammering a surfcaster onto his back, then drawing him down in a backwash to flounder helplessly in deep water, where his garments will draw him under in seconds to drown.

On rockbound shores one step can cause a person to lose his footing, be inundated by a violent surf, then end up pounded mercilessly against the stones.

For those who gather on the edge of tiderips, sudden dropoffs wait downtide for the person who loses his footing or is suddenly swept from the safety of the bar by increasing currents or a maverick wave.

Just to show you how varied the dangers can be, who ever heard of being lost at sea while wading? I have.

While bait fishing sea worms one night on Nauset Beach's Long Bar in a thick fog, I walked a couple of hundred feet in low-tide shallows to cast, turned to free spool line to sand spikes, and couldn't determine in the gray darkness in which direction to go to use those sand spikes.

But the scariest incident of being lost while shore fishing was with Red Hudson at Chatham Inlet during my rod-and-reel commercial fishing days. He and I were casting plugs into the early rising tide, up to the top of our waders, stringing schoolies onto ropes attached to our wader belts. No moon, thick fog. We were standing parallel to the beach, maybe 30 feet apart. After fighting each fish, we would turn our backs to the rip, then remove the hooks and string the fish up. If a particular bass was difficult to remove, we illuminated our neck lights to do it; however, I found that each time I used the light it had the effect of creating vertigo, where I stumbled in the deep water momentarily unable to judge what direction to cast to. Pausing to hear Red's reel or the swish of his cast, I could determine where he was, envision him in his usual position, then orient myself for the next cast.

One of the times I couldn't locate Red, didn't know where

to cast, and went flush at the notion that if I didn't know where to cast, I certainly didn't know where shore was. Worse, when I called for him there was no answer. I later learned that Red could hear me but had a small flashlight in his mouth, as he was putting fish away. It was a long five minutes with me yelling, "Hey, Red!" at the top of my lungs before he answered calmly.

For all that I've said about the hazards of the beach, it is a wonder that there are not more deaths while surf fishing. About the most historically dangerous spot that I know of is Narragansett, Rhode Island, where an average of about one person is killed per year, and only about half are surfcasters. A surfman died on the south Cape a couple of years ago in full daylight; other than the fact that he lacked experience, few details are available as to the cause.

We take the space to address death here, but injury presents too many possibilities for a full and effective treatment. Stripers are spiny, and their dorsal can penetrate unsuspecting surfcasters who try to cradle a big fish in their arms while a wild surf batters them about. Bluefish have teeth backed by the power to tighten their jaws enough to amputate an unsuspecting hand.

Of course accidents will happen, but I'm convinced that the hazards that relate to our game are so obvious that good safety practice becomes a case of listening to one's fears. Certainly, the beach is fearsome enough a place—particularly in darkness—to repeatedly remind its transgressors of impending danger. The water pushes you back to where you feel comfortable, and where you feel right is usually considerably higher than you have to be.

COMPULSIVE SURFCASTERS

Perhaps the biggest hazard of all lurks within ourselves, given that most of us surfcasters have a strong tendency to fish far more than we should. That may sound like a strange thing to say here, if you view getting out there as something you are always trying to squeeze bits out of the clock for, deriving a heightened sense of well-being when you can relax a bit near the water. On the other hand, a great many anglers, particularly stripermen, have a compulsive need to be there, going beyond that little self-indulgence that we all feel we owe ourselves.

This compulsion probably springs in part from some deep-seated inner fear that a major event—a large number of stripers moving into an area or a moderate take of big fish—is liable to happen without us. I can personally testify that people who overly commit themselves to chasing bass endure seven months of short rest annually, sleeping with one eye open. When sportfishing gets to that point, it isn't any good for anybody. Any time you catch yourself moving your spoon through the corn flakes at different levels, varying its speed, it may be time to question your priorities. There are, after all, other things in life.

I might have gotten to know more about such things if, thirty years ago, I hadn't gotten into the habit of spending Friday nights at the shore. There was a small gang of us, all in our twenties, who used to fill a car with gear and enthusiasm. For this I always spent Thursday evening with charts and maps to lay out a plan for us. The boys let me do the planning because I *seemed* to know what I was doing, when I really knew little about striped bass.

In season none of us ever missed a Friday night until the second year when two of the regulars quit rather mysteriously; the rumor was wives. You couldn't blame them—these safaris were so brutal that the rest of the weekend was shot. What spouse is going to put up with that as a steady diet? Worse, if Friday night was productive, most of us would roll the dice again Saturday. Apparently the compulsion gets to a point where everything else in your life starts to give way under the strain. By late in the second year all that was left of the bunch was my brother, Norman, and one other. I think the notion that we might be overdoing things came to me ei-

There are other things in life besides fishing the striper surf. Let me see . . . .

ther the morning we slept on the side of the road 8 miles from home, awakening with flies crawling in our nostrils; or the sunrise we were dying for a beer. There are only two kinds of folks looking for a drink at 6:00 A.M.: compulsive drinkers and compulsive surfcasters. If you have the uneasy feeling that you are being watched while waiting for a downtown bar to open, maybe you shouldn't be there. Norman, an off-duty police officer, explained to the bartender that we didn't want breakfast—an egg in the beer or a shot in the tomato juice—that ours was a nightcap. So much for bedtime.

I've known a long list of stripermen who ruined their marriages because of fishing. For one thing, the season is too long. It is not like salmon fishing, where there are a few good weeks in a river; nor is it comparable to deer hunting, say a month in fall on the outside. Striper anglers begin in April and quit in November, providing that winter sets in early.

Consider, too, the influence that striper fishing has upon careers. We have no studies to support it, but I'll bet that few stripermen are carrying much sick leave on the books. Remember anglers who hit the shore Saturday night if Friday night was hot? What do you think a compulsive angler does when Saturday night was good fishing as well? The rationale—or should I have said logic?—is that who knows when fishing will be this good again? Between the individuals who don't know when to quit and those who can't wait, Mondays and Fridays can be awfully quiet at work. I even know a number of young men, who should have been at the height of their professional development who just quit working and walked away to sleep in the back of a truck for the rest of the season. Some had angles that helped to keep body and soul together—unemployment or early pensions for some perceived ailment—but that stuff either runs out, or the pensions, eaten up by inflation during the years I speak of here, amount to poverty. These men knew all these things, but the good life on the sand, under the stars, the promise of high drama, was a drug.

Another trap of the Striper Coast that used to take place in my time was going professional. The rod-and-reel commercial has since been legislated out of existence, what with striper conservation and PCB bans on the sale of bass. Before all that, the money fishermen fit this discussion nicely. I knew a union carpenter who gave up some good folding green and group insurance to fish stripers commercially. As the best striper boatman I ever knew, he doubled his nail-banging pay prowling the seas between Fisher's Island Race in New York and Charlestown, Rhode Island. Yes, he lived some platinum nights pounding the rivets out of his Starcraft. His skills in taking linesides, his intimacy with a deadly sea, his total obsession with conditions, fish, and their interrelationship haunted his every waking moment and most of what little he slept. In the long run it never led to anything. He had to be there all the time because he apparently felt that if he couldn't control either the obsession or the compulsion, he might as well get paid for it.

Others who did the same thing met with less success; that is, if we measure success in some balance between how happy a person is and how much money he is making doing it. People caught up this way are truly victims of the compulsion to fish for stripers, and what is forgotten is that it is supposed to be a game like grouse hunting or skeet shooting. We like straying with our examples because you, dear reader, should recognize that there are other things.

Twenty years ago I fished Westport, Massachusetts, with a gentleman who kept every stick of his striper tackle hidden in the trunk of his car. He once confided to me that he would love a one-piece surf rod, but he had to keep it out of sight of his neighbors, that he didn't want them to know he was going fishing. Unmarried, he had total freedom, a comfortable job, and no one to answer to. He fished so much—seven nights a week season long—that it actually embarrassed him for anyone to know that he was that much of a surfcasting junkie. He simply didn't want to have to talk about it with anybody. His embarrassment about his inability to control the compulsion to be fishing tells us he knew the surf-fishing thing had gone too far. While I never understood his behavior then, I have since known enough of his ilk and suffered the malady myself enough to recognize the symptoms.

One summer on the Cape a few years ago, when we had been taking an incredible number of big stripers, I was made to take a long look at myself. While the fishing had been good, it had been brutally hard. The only advantage that we had was that we knew the fish were going to make a landfall somewhere on 30 miles of beach before sunrise. Fishing two hours on Race Point at low tide, we then hurried east to test a few points while the tide was making. It was cast, run, and analyze; look for bait, note the wind, night after night, week after week. My hands ached from small infections that I had gotten handling bass, salt irritating each tiny wound. Having lost fifteen pounds in two months, I was haggard and gaunt. This night of which I speak, a midtide windshift to the nor'west ruined what had been a productive itinerary, causing us to fall into our bunks after midnight in total exhaustion.

I've been known to sleep if satisfied that I've kept the beach honest. I thought that all possibilities had been covered when, with a sleeping bag pulled up around my neck, I felt a gentle breeze complete the checklist of universal surfcaster sleep aids. Before long came that familiar, gnawing sense taunting some otherwise unreachable part of my mind, accusing me of not having fished the beach right, not having allowed for the wind change. It was as though a part of me was still at work on some yet-unsolved problem, while my body and conscious mind sought to sleep. While I have no notions about extrasensory perception, something caused my eyes to open and made me see that a waxing moon had risen. And though I forced my eyes shut, the compulsion to run the beach had flooded my consciousness.

Whipping the family buggy east along the water line past barren dunes and sliding whitecaps, I went at the pleasure of some indiscernible, inscrutable urgency, that said, "They are doing it without you!" Then, 12 miles from our camper, while rounding a prominent point that keeps Highland Light from view, I saw all the darkened buggies gathered at a hole with one surfman hurrying a big striper to the shadow of his vehicle. Running down to the water, I could see the many drag marks: sure evidence of a kill. Yet all the anglers had retreated to their buggies, and my eel came back each time unmolested. I was too late.

I was exasperated at having misjudged a situation I had come to pride myself on conquering: Striped bass were not going to feed in the Cape Cod surf without me.

Of course, with the inevitable wisdom of age, I now recognize that you can't be everywhere and anticipate everything, that you have to draw the line. Otherwise you end up with surf rods that fish you and no other life.

⪜ Memorable Places and Times ⪜

Inland bass fishermen call them "honey holes," salmon and trout fishermen call them "lies"; but we of the striper surf, probably because our craft is newer and not steeped in tradition, have yet to coin a name for those special places where, unaccountably, stripers love to hole up.

There have been so many special striper places in my life that there are few beaches, jetties, or estuaries that I can probe that don't bring each one of them right to the fore of my mind. At times they pop into my consciousness en route—or if they're of lesser status, soon after I start fishing. I'm not talking about the big, overgeneralized places like Montauk or Narragansett, but the little specifics: within 5 yards, the left side of a river rock on a falling tide or the slough of some obscure bar where foam breaks on a coming tide. For such a spot to earn space in my mind, it must have given up an occasional bass scant feet from where it did last, with a measure of repeatability, while dead water around it remained fishless.

Naturally these "steadies" rely upon a change or break in the structure of a particular area, however subtle. At low tide at Cape Cod's Race Point, the bottom is flat to the eye. You are not likely to see the barely discernible impressions there that set one small yardage apart from another. Still, during a raging onshore sou'west, if you cast a 400-yard stretch of the

Race shore, there is one place where a wind-disturbed sea kicks up differently than it does anywhere else there. If you didn't already know the bottom, you would swear that no reason exists for this rogue area; after all, the bottom appears no different. Yet if a few inches of tide have risen, there is an impression there, however faint. Because of it your plug will swing harder to the north by 10 degrees than it does along the rest of the beach. Of course, this is something that you would never notice unless you became analytical about it, and you wouldn't do that unless you noticed that you were catching more stripers while standing there than in any other set of boot prints on the beach.

That is not to say that where a caster stands is the whole story. Indeed, we would have to include how far one casts the plug, how much of the plug's action is left to the whim of the tide, and just how hard the wind is blowing. We learn these things, as they relate to that particular spot, quite by accident, but we would be fools indeed to forget them. So often, so many seasons, I have slid a Rebel or Bomber past that "drop" to have it taken inches, it seemed, from where it had happened before. Blitzy nights, when others were making ten casts for a contact, you could hook up on each cast until you stuck every fish that was using the place. Then, if you rested it, you could come back and start a few more bass. One night I was seen taking so many stripers from that spot that the following night a fellow staked it out with bait rods, both to fish it and preclude anyone else—particularly me—from using it. That is one reason we share such knowledge only with those we love.

Along the easterly facing Outer Cape beach is a 100-yard stretch where the buggy track is always washed away. Under a bright sun you can see the emerald hue of a hole that is more prominent than any of the others that an astute observer might find. Thankfully, beach vehicles are diverted around the spot for safety reasons, and as a consequence many don't know it is there. They don't know that beach washouts are always accompanied by holes and that holes hold bass; indeed, the place appears to have so much promise that it is only a case of determining which tide is best. Some years the hole there does not form, but when it does you can fish every prominent spot along the beach without ever locating stripers. Then you can cast each yard of the hole and usually find fish. It is simply the best place to be. In the heyday of big stripers, the late seventies, my wife and I once landed twenty-five fish over 35 pounds; there were many, many lesser nights, and I once took a 50-pound-plus there. The edges of the hole were best, affirming the notion that the fish were ambushing bait as it drifted over the shallower bars. Tide depending, most of the linesides favored the downtide edge; but midtide on a moon, the water there back-eddies, thus turning around twice in a six-hour period, causing the bass to shift more than they would anywhere else. I also think the fish were just doing a lot of plain, old-fashioned hanging around. It was an intriguing spot, with a yield far outdistancing its promise. You wouldn't want a place to look as good as it really is anyway, because angling pressure would only destroy it. I remember so many neat-looking honey holes we've fished in the past that could make even a budding novice pant, yet they wouldn't give up a fish if ole King Neptune himself was working it.

Jigging the bottom of fast-water runs can be a very productive technique for stripers. The reason is that there isn't anything else made among artificials that will get through the currents to where stripers can acquire some rest from the push of water. But the niftiest thing of all about jigging fast water is that few others do it. Many don't know how or don't want to risk tackle with the bottom, or they dislike the laborious speed of casting a jig and have it swing and finish its drift within seconds. Consequently, the best tiderips in the territory are fished in a sluffed-over way. There are a number of jetties in Rhode Island that nightly entertain crowds of surfcasters, more so on weekends. Yet these breachways are not jigged along their more productive insides. Many anglers believe that the water is too fast for a striper to hold in. At such places you are apt to find a stray fish holding anywhere. Thus a methodical "farming" of the bottom should have your jig passing every few feet in order to give every striper a fair shot at pulling you off the slick rocks from which you are casting. Naturally, no regular who makes it a point of working such places would ever put in much time without learning that there are choice chunks of real estate that inexplicably appeal to the fishes. You don't have to know why. I don't know anyway.

One such spot lies in a narrowing point between two jetties where the water truly accelerates. Midtide the water hisses white through there with such a will that you have to cast 40 feet above in order for a 3-ounce bucktail to pass at nose height to a waiting striper. It is kind of a place of the heart. I've looked at it, squinting through polaroids in the day, and noticed that a good-size rock is there. Maybe the rock does something to create a neutral hydro for a bass to lie comfortably in the accidental magic of swirling water. I am certain, however, that if only one bass is going to show between those jetties to feed she is going to take that particular hold. When the jig stops it is either she or the rock, but rocks don't writhe. There is something special about going to a place, in the face of a seeming boundlessness of an ocean, and catching a fish as though you knew all the time she would be there—cashing in the chips of experience. Now that stripers are coming back, and I have every reason to believe that they are, there seem to be enough bass to go around, but not the easy ones.

CHILDREN FISHING

Some of the most memorable times occur when fishing with children. They are willing participants and take to fishing quickly. Kids love to collect, hunger to contribute, thirst to reach back to some basic, inner drive. Man as a species has many more years as a food gatherer on this planet than he does as a shopper who selects his prepackaged foods. I am convinced that the agrarian tendency is so ingrained in all of us that any food-gathering activities are instinctive. Among older people, however, who have had time to formulate opinions about themselves and the world around them, social influences have suppressed such natural incentives. While adults debate the wisdom of walking along a beach after dark or in the rain, children will participate without question. While parents quantify food yield against time engaged, our unfettered children take part enthusiastically, free of the social constraints—the learned behavior of age—that so inhibit their parents. Watch children gathering fruit in a huff of unharnessed delight, and you will realize how little time has passed since man ceased to provide for his own needs. So it is with tossing a line into the sea in the hope of bringing something out.

All children like fishing before they start. It is what you expose them to after they begin that will determine whether or not they continue. Never try to cram the whole thing into a student too quickly. We walk a fine line here where, fun as learning may be, frustrations can be crushing and may jeopardize the whole mission. Teach casting in the day under the most favorable conditions; later you can add the complications that we all know exist in the real surfcasting world. Early fishing should be easy, productive, and safe. This is best accomplished by using bait where the fishing is good (preferably for an easier species than stripers) for something that the child can take home and enjoy at the table. By doing this you utilize those natural agrarian incentives.

While a child is never too old to learn fishing, there are incidents where they can be started at too early an age. Yes, it may contribute to the overall mission for some exposure to take place as a toddler, but I would not embark upon any serious teaching until the age of seven. By then the youngster is capable of learning casting, baiting a hook, and bringing in a struggling gamefish. Many parents will be astounded at how quickly these young neophytes can learn such activities. Educators have long known that motivation is the key to the instructional process; as a parent, you will find this element of

Great men gather where the great fish are.

learning built in.

During the first years of exposure, the child's interest level and performance do not vary along sexual lines. Having raised three daughters and a son, we saw no difference in their enthusiasm. However, the absence of a role model of the same sex does sometimes impede a girl's interest as she grows up. Still, I would not hesitate to introduce fishing to a young girl, permitting her to make her own judgments about it.

The joys of having a child who comes along fishing are self-evident. Except for a brief and somewhat painful period, when a youngster's interests are biologically shaken between sixteen and twenty years old, the filial relationship is heightened for a lifetime. My efforts to teach our children fishing, along with a wife and mother who fishes with plugs, bait, and flies, have made us a fishing family.

In our home there is not a day that passes when fishing doesn't find its way into the conversation. We all are casters and all have a tender memory of our greatest angling accomplishments. The subjects of who is catching what and where stripers are hanging out often take precedence over all but the most dire international developments. Our children are now long grown, some with kids of their own, spread from Maine to Maryland. Wherever they have been they have always looked upon water with more than a passing interest.

PART TWO

SURF TACKLE
AND EQUIPMENT

Spinning Gear

It would hardly seem necessary to create a distinction between spinning and other types of equipment: Nearly 100 percent of the equipment in use is spinning, and this has been the case throughout the thirty years that I have been in the surf. The distinction is necessary, though, if we are to later address alternative methods.

I do not recall how long it took me to learn casting with this equipment, but I do know that I was able to teach our children enough about casting in twenty minutes to have them effectively surf fishing. The little nuances—casting overly light lures, lashing a plug into a headwind, spot casting, and learning to do these things in the dark—take a little longer. These are learned as you go along, and the process of becoming familiar with your equipment can be a delightful enhancement to the joys of surf fishing. We emphasize that casting is probably the easiest aspect of the sport as long as the person chooses spinning tackle.

In the casting world the high surf requires about the heaviest spinning tackle made. Unlike inland fishing, the surf rod is cast with two hands that are swung with a force about equal to that used in hitting a ball in baseball or a tee shot in golf. That can represent a considerable expenditure of energy when repeated for many hours, so you'll want to select the most comfortable and efficient equipment that will contribute greater distances with less expended energy.

In the selection of casting tackle, three things must be closely scrutinized to achieve an optimum efficiency in casting: the overall weight of the rod-and-reel combination, the length of the rod and its action, and line strength.

The average surf rod–and-reel combination should weigh around 2¼ pounds, give or take ounces, but a badly chosen outfit could weigh as much as ½ pound over that. This added weight does nothing to enhance the overall performance of the equipment. With that simple consideration out of the way, the complexities of rod-length choice and rod action need greater elaboration.

Most people will find a rod length of 9 feet suitable. No adjustments are required for individual physical characteristics, because the variation in height from a short person to a tall one is so slight, at least for the selection of a surf rod, that it is a dispensable factor. We learned this when ordering a custom rod for our ten-year-old son, when we found that he was only 10 percent shorter than a adult. And he is still fishing with the rod twenty-two years later! *Most* of the surf rods on the market are overly long, with offers of 10 to 12 feet and even longer. It is both unnecessary and cumbersome to engage such abominable equipment. Overly long rods convey excessive forces to the caster, are resistant to wind, and contribute unnecessary weight. I don't blame the manufacturers for this. It is the fault of demand, because so many surfcasters believe that longer rods produce longer casts.

A rod's action depends upon the type of fishing. Rods used for bait fishing, where large sinkers and baits might be used, or those used to work popping plugs or rigged eels, should be on the stiffer side. Conversely, those casting lighter-weight swimming plugs, down to ½ ounce, should be of light action. Of course, given one rod, I would choose a medium action for all of these applications.

The size and type of guides on a surf rod will affect both the cast and the all important term life of the rod. The first guide above the reel should be as close in size as possible to that of the reel's spool. It should *ideally* be as large, but that's rarely attainable. I know of a few production rods made by the big manufacturers that offer a suitable first guide. They know better, but a large first guide (as well as offering rods in one piece) affects their ability to efficiently ship large quantities. For this reason, so-called custom surf rods have flourished on the Striper Coast. Above the first collector guide, two guides will experience the most wear from the miles of monofilament that are run across them: the tip and last guide. These are often made of chrome and will exhibit minute grooves, when examined with a jeweler's loop, by the end of their first season. Once these grooves begin to take hold, line damage is certain to have already resulted. Ideally, all guides would be fitted with a ceramic running surface, except for the first, largest guide.

The answer to optimum line size is simple: 20-pound test. It is unwise, particularly for the beginning surfcaster, to use anything but the largest line when applied to the perfect, heavy surf spinning equipment. The size alone of trophy striped bass would dictate that, but there is more. Casting distance is controlled by the amount of depletion that takes place on the spool during the cast. A line of 15 pounds, while it is 25 percent weaker, is only 15 percent smaller; thus, there is poor economy in the trade-off. Casts will get noticeably longer with 12-pound test, but the loss in strength places the fisherman at a disadvantage. In the other direction, 25-pound test so encumbers casting distances and so reduces the choices of suitable weights that it is impractical in all but the most specialized applications: those in which the caster is certain ahead of time that he or she will be casting a heavy weight a short distance for known large fish. We recommend 20-pound line simply because all other sizes are fraught with difficulty.

SPINNING REELS

Earlier we talked about the influence of spool depletion upon casting distances; for this reason, the caster should be equipped with a reel of the largest possible spool size. This is determined by the diameter of the spool, not its purported capacity, though no surf spinning reel filled with 20-pound line should hold less than 200 yards. Better reels have skirted spools, which protect working parts from salt and sand intrusion and are less likely to have line foul under the spool. Serious surfcasters should always have an extra spool for their chosen reel, as it is the best protection against the most likely equipment problems. Line can be damaged, leaving an overly depleted spool after it is cut back. The standard retrieve for right-handed casters is left hand. Gear ratios—the number of turns that occur for each turn of the handle—should be about as large as available, because a high ratio brings a lure or bait in quicker during that period when it has been determined that it is no longer fishing. Also, fast ratios make popper-plug fishing a joy; however, the trade-off of such rapid retrieves is that the angler should be conscious of this on nights when moby linesides are smashing slow-swimming plugs.

I do not believe that casting can be taught in the pages of a book, but there is one pearl of advice that I would offer any surfcaster, including many who have heaved lures into the saltchuck for as long as I have. Either never form—or break—the habit of casting a lure with 2 feet or less trailing from the tip. Such casting habits unnecessarily inhibit the application of force. When a lure is cast with a longer drop from the tip, a greater amount of centrifugal force can be applied by the caster. Using a 9-foot rod with a 2-foot drop, the caster is swinging the weight through an arc of 11 feet, but the caster with a 7-foot drop—about from the tip down to the reel—is moving his or hers through a 16-foot arc with the same amount of expended effort; so it is possible to outcast your counterparts with ease, while they lunge and grunt mightily. You need only look at competition distance casters going through their thing to recognize what is needed to put a lure into blue water. They, of course, both grunt and apply good physics to their craft. Such long trails when casting will feel a bit unwieldy at first, but they are worth perfecting when you consider the long-term and nightlong benefits. Good surfcasting is an endurance game, and one must be miserly about effort, particularly if there is nothing to gain.

Longer rods don't necessarily lead to longer casts.

LIGHT-TACKLE SPINNING

There is notable sport in casting small, half-ounce plugs with 10- or 12-pound line using a one-handed rod. This is the case particularly if small bass are known to be in an area or if the fisherman is working a tidal estuary. Indeed, such tackle calls upon all of the surfcaster's skills to fight and land larger specimens, say, more than 20 pounds. And a 5-inch Rebel/Red-Fin–type swimmer, which so perfectly balances out with such "schoolie tackle," is a formidably effective way to coax a brute lineside into taking. It certainly elevates the level of spin fishing to a higher order of sportfishing. When an angler is confronted with such a fish using this equipment, it is not unusual to be engaged for half an hour or more. Our son, Dick, landed a 40-pounder on such tackle when he was ten years old.

One of the joys of such equipment is the variety of rods—developed for Great Lakes steelheading—that have come to the market from the big tackle companies. All offer graphite, two-piece models of 7 or 8 feet with ceramic guides that, accident that it might be, are both perfect for the mission of light spinning and dwarf any efforts that "custom" rod makers in scattered shops around the Striper Coast might put forth. For all that can be said about the virtue of custom-made, full-size surf rods, the same can be said of schoolie tackle from the big-name tackle companies.

Before any surfcaster, even those of you with a moderate wealth of surfcasting experience, sets out to take on a big striped bass, be forewarned that such a fish is not beaten by simply waiting it out with a mile of line. We have lost many trophy linesides when, after changing direction in the fight, they managed a coil of line around their bodies. It is an easy thing for a big fish to do when it is allowed its head, which is a necessity with light tackle. Once such gossamer thin lines find their way under one of the many quarter-sized scales that armor-plate a striper's body, the flexing of that body during violent efforts to swim off will so damage the mono as to render its remaining strength unworkable. That's why it's possible to fight such a fish and survive great forces early in the contact, then suddenly have your line go limp from the break-off when no force at all was exerted later.

Spinning tackle is popular because it can be used for a wide range of lure weights and is a necessity because it is both easy to use and will deliver light—down to half-ounce—plugs with relative ease. It is first choice with a majority of surfcasters, and it should be yours.

≈ "Conventional" Surf Fishing ≈

I n truth, there is nothing conventional in the use of revolving—sometimes called bait-casting—reels in surf fishing. I'll guess that less than 5 percent of surfcasters use the tackle at all, though there are, on a limited regional basis, a few spots that enjoy slightly higher application of the tackle. The term "conventional" is left over from the time when spinning gear made its debut and was used as a means to differentiate between the two. Naturally, the advent of spinning gave rise to friendly disputes over the merits of each. Time indicates that the results are in and that spinning has won more widespread acceptance; however, common perceptions and inaccuracies about conventional tackle still linger. Deciding exactly when the whole thing started is no small part of the dispute.

A few things about time and tackle: I remember drawing a crowd on the rocks of Narragansett, Rhode Island, while fishing revolving spool, because none of the surfcasters there had ever seen it in use; the year was 1968. In 1961 I fished in a Charlestown blitz where the beach was lined with surfmen for a mile east to Green Hill; only one angler was fishing conventional, and I didn't even own one at the time.

Obviously, then, widespread use of spinning predates even my own surfcasting. My guess is that the dispute was at full height during the midfifties, when I was in high school.

We'll elaborate below upon the elements of this dispute. Proponents of both types of tackle have naturally always felt that theirs was better for use in surf fishing. We address these issues with the full knowledge that one has always been free to fish with whatever one chooses. More importantly, the issues themselves form the basis for this section on conventional fishing as a means to instruct upon the merits and weaknesses of both.

PROS AND CONS

In the earlier section on spinning, you will recall that 20-pound test was my advised upper limit in line strength. In conventional fishing that strength is the lower limit; in fact, a surfcaster can go as high as 50 pound with the old-time gear. The application of such high-strength lines acts as a solution to a number of surfcasting problems: 1) fishing and fighting large stripers in powerful tiderips; 2) coping with groups of other anglers who are either unwilling or too excited to yield to an angler who is fighting a fish; 3) controlling big fish from nosing themselves into a variety of obstructions to rid themselves of a tormenting line; 4) more effectively battling world-class trophy fish where the greatest percentage of losses occurs when spinning tackle is used (let's place the size of such fish at 50 pounds and up); 5) casting and retrieving very heavy lures and sinker bait combinations; and 6) distance.

Now the price. Conventional reels are far and away more difficult to cast and require weeks of practice to learn. Further, if you want to utilize the strength advantage, you'll find that they cast light lures poorly. Line must be retrieved level on the spool (in most cases), and learning to do this in the dark so as to have the skill a second nature sometimes requires years; thus, when we take these difficulties into account, the degree of expertise required to utilize conventional tackle tells us that it is no small wonder that nearly everyone is fishing spinning gear. Much of this is widely known, and, as a consequence, its use has carried with it a certain implied level of expertise—sort of making it the "tackle of the pros." I hasten to point out that this social abomination is neither of my making, nor is it my intention to perpetuate such one-up notions. The perception was there when I started surfcasting, and I am powerless to stop it, probably because there is some basis in fact.

One consequence of that implied expertise is that there are a lot of would-be pros who fish with it badly. Such behavior, in my view, is a meaningless subversion of the equipment practiced by a minority who pay each painful night with bleeding thumbs and screeching backlashes. Let's get back to the reasons why the technique is used.

RODS

Properly applied, this tackle should be taking up where spinning tackle leaves off. The word is heavy. Ideal rods should be a trifle longer than those used in spinning, say 9½ feet, but their action should be just short of that of a pool cue for casting baits and lures from 4 ounces up to 10. (An example of 10 ounces might be a 6- or 8-ounce sinker with a chunk bait.) Again we must hail the small custom shops of the Striper Coast for being the only ones capable of providing such rods. Guides must be of either Carboloy or ceramic to withstand line wear. Reel seats should not even exist on such conventional rods, because all of the reels offered come equipped for clamping to the blank. Tubular glass remains first choice at this writing, because to my knowledge no one in the industry has ever built a graphite blank that is stiff enough for the mission of delivering the weights of which we speak.

CONVENTIONAL REELS

The Penn squidder has dominated conventional reel use for at least fifty years. We are tempted here to label it the M1 of

If you can get used to it, cast with a longer trail from the tip of your rod.

conventional casting, because it is the bulwark of this tackle. I have models that have been with me for twenty-five years through the fruits of my own ability to maintain and repair them. Along with being about the lowest-priced reels available, it is a certainty that with the help of factory maintenance, which is necessary for all equipment, they could last your lifetime. The demise of the squidder, if not here already, will come with the advent of improved state-of-the-art conventional reels, however. Thus, while we sing praises for the squidder, there are now reels on the market, one made by Penn in the form of a 980 Mag-Force, which exceed the squidder's performance. Reels that came on the market in the mideighties are easier to use and go an impressive distance toward allaying the old curses of difficulty and backlashing. Even some of the level-wind models would aid the neophyte in tackle transitions, in spite of arguments that exaggerate the loss of distance.

LINES

Conventional casting lines should take up where spinning lines leave off: 30-pound-test mono. Naturally, as with the spinning, lighter lines cast better, but the nearer we get to 20-pound test, the less justification remains for using conventional tackle. With this line strength you should be able to cast all but the lightest lures thrown in spinning: 1½ to 4 ounces. Where distance requirements are not important, it is possible to utilize 40-pound mono with plugs and baits 3 ounces up. In specialized applications where moby fish are worked up close, I have even resorted to 50-pound mono. Two examples come to mind in the application of this highest strength: huge bucktail jigs from bridges and also in the breachways of Rhode Island when the tide was roaring through. You will note that where mono is concerned, there is an enlarging group of trade-offs in place as the mono's size increases. But there is a solution to this.

Time was when a variety of braided lines were offered, but lowered market acceptance and some advances have reduced this to one line: Cortland braided micron. Even this braid—a formulation of Dacron and Teflon—is marketed as "trolling line," though I am sure it was developed for casting. Braid is more supple, thus more forgiving to those who are backlash prone. When used in 45-pound test, it is possible for the surf-caster to utilize plugs or eels as light as 1½ ounces and as heavy as 4. With this enlarged range of weight utilizations, without strength trade-offs, you can do with a single braided line, the one described above, with 30-, 40-, or 50-pound mono.

Braided line is horrifically abrasive, particularly after some of the lube Teflon has worn away. By your second night of casting, there will be a groove in the level-wind thumb of your left hand. Worse, the discomfort heightens as the groove penetrates each layer of skin, salt finding its way, so you need to tape your left thumb before each night of fishing and on long nights replace this tape midway, because it also grooves from the line's abrasion. In spite of such difficulties, I would still recommend braid for anyone who wants a backlash-free night and strength with a variety of lure weights.

To avoid spooking fish, I am inclined to avoid braided line fished too close to bait or lure. I would avoid tying the braid direct, but if one were to utilize the long trail from tip to lure when casting, as mentioned in the spinning gear section (pages 91–97), 6 feet of 40- or 50-pound mono could be placed between the line and lure, but tied to a small barrel for a strong connection. I have known some surfmen to splice mono to braid back to the reel, a distance of about 12 feet; however, this knot is hammered at the guides on every cast, and I have known many to break off at that very point.

Braid is water resistant in that it is influenced more by water motion than is mono; thus, one would be ill advised to fish bottom with a sinker using braid, as the surf tends to push it about, and currents will cause a sinker to drag mercilessly. The line's true advantage lies in casting and retrieving as is done with plugging or eel fishing. Use mono to fish bottom.

Whatever your line choice, the reel should be capable of holding a minimum of 160 yards.

CONVENTIONAL VS. SPINNING

Contrary to almost universal choices, my own surfcasting is 94 percent conventional, 5 percent fly fishing, and 1 percent spinning. I now do so little spinning that my qualifications to elaborate upon it could easily be brought into question. This is, of course, because the revolving spool meets all my surfcasting needs. Still, I would urge caution to anyone making choices and categorically advise against starting out surfcasting with "conventional" tackle. Spinning is far easier, and there are too many other things a surfcaster must learn rather than be encumbered with mechanics when other options are available. The transition to a different type of tackle should come about slowly, later in a caster's development, and always with a spinning outfit at the ready to save a night of fishing.

⇒ *Fly Fishing* ⇒

For a number of practical reasons, the striper surf is no place to take up fly fishing. The nuances of the sport are more demanding than any other, and, even with the fly, we are still surfcasting here, which means that it must be done at night—no time for a person to be learning. Surfcasting is difficult enough without adding a method that is foreign to the angler. On the other hand, any fisherman already familiar with fly fishing from fresh water should never overlook its advantages.

At first the thought of taking stripers on a fly may seem a little intimidating, and there may be good reason if light, bendable rods do that to you. Concern for breaking off should not be a worry, however, because a fly caster can use a leader that tests as large as that of 20-pound spinning gear. Personally, I rarely go under 15; thus, while fly rods do go into scarier bends than our more traditional tackle when fish are on, chances of breaking off are no greater and probably less.

The best argument for fly fishing for stripers lies in the fly itself. In our waters the sand eel, with its long, slim body build, is popular forage bait. While these can be found in deep water, they are more likely to dig in along our beaches. Most striper anglers have learned that any artificial that is small and slim will look enough like a sand eel to take a

A streamer made of white-saddle hackle does a notable job of simulating a sand eel.

greater share of bass than the fat plugs. You need only look at the number and variety of Rebels, Redfins, Bombers, Hellcats, and Rapalas in widespread spinning use along our shores, to recognize that the use of this family of plugs is related to its similarity in appearance with sand eels. Even the smallest of these plugs, however, is both inaccurate in size proportion and overactive in swimming action to be a true look-alike to the sand eel. There is not a plug made that has a body one-twelfth as deep as it is long, slender enough to match the natural animal. Mature sand eels run 4 to 6 inches, on average, and 5-inch bait fish are only ⅜ inch round at their widest point. Properly tied, the fly comes closer both in size and proportion.

Sand-eel flies should be long and thin, wispy, almost transparent, like the real sand eel. For that reason we use saddle hackle feathers of 4 to 6 inches. The five to eight feathers are tied at the throat of a Mustad 34007 hook in a 2/0 size. It is neither necessary nor desirable to utilize any other materials. Building up the body with bucktail tends to overly thicken it, adding weight and water absorption, which can impede the fly's effectiveness. While it would do no harm to use darker colors along the flanks and top of the fly to enhance imitation, I have never observed any heightened effectiveness by such touches of realism. The striper's angle of attack remains from below, nearly always in darkness. Use a stainless hook, because any other will corrode after one use, staining the feathers.

Never make the mistake of thinking that fly fishing for stripers is schoolie fishing. Of course, that could be the case if the fish at hand are running on the small side. But any seasoned striper angler knows that the surprise of a larger fish is just as inevitable while fly fishing as it is using other methods. There are even cases when fish, of any size, will take the fly while forsaking all other offers. I began experiencing this as soon as I started.

The most spectacular incident took place many years later at Race Point. We had come upon a spread of very large bass in the shallows, their tails barely breaking the surface as they rooted on the bottom for sand eels. None of the standard surf-casting methods enumerated in this book would move a single fish, and there were dozens of good men trying. Out of sheer frustration, I pulled my salmon rod down off the top of the buggy with a back-of-the-mind feeling that it would do no better, but I couldn't lose. Stripping the fly past a working fish in vain, my next effort passed it deeper at a height that I hoped was scratching the sand. The striper seized it and just went right on digging for more. It was not until I hauled back violently that the thing took off, screaming into the backing in seconds. As you might expect, it took a few minutes to get the brute close enough to the beach for gaffing.

A few minutes later I found another fish working the same way and similarly coaxed it to the take. The fish were similar in size, only this one was able to run the backing deeper, presenting significant fighting differences. For one thing the line-side would lunge, setting the reel into a violent spin, yet when I tightened the drag slightly, it seemed to stick, raising dangerous forces upon the leader. The one that was on the beach weighed 43 pounds, and the one on the line intimidated my equipment past anything I had just experienced. We cannot be certain that it necessarily was larger, however, because the tide was changing and the Race current, where my fish was, was building. Whatever the reason, scant yards from its end, the backing backlashed on a violent run, cutting itself at the spool.

FLY REELS

A valuable lesson to be learned from this is that you cannot ever have too good a reel for dealing with big, fly-caught stripers. The effective range of the drag system has to be designed for the kind of forces that both spinning and conventional surf reels already have. Unfortunately, state of the art for big-game fly fishing is slightly behind that of other means. It is not enough to simply pay a lot of money for a reel that will hold a #10 weight forward, saltwater tapered line and 200 yards of backing. I've already done that for reels with drags that will not tighten enough to snub a moderate striper down. Worse, we again deal with trade-offs. The reel that you want is available, but it will weigh far more than it should, and the weight of a fly reel can kill your casting arm.

To summarize, any reel light enough to be suitable will not

For seasoned fly fishermen, there is no better way to catch stripers.

have a drag with a proper or heavy enough range of forces for big stripers. Those that do a yeoman's job will kill your arm. There is greater efficiency in multiplying fly reels, those that turn more times than that of the crank. But the tradition of "single action" fly reels, which wind one turn of line for one crank, is, after all, part of the sport.

SALTY FLY RODS

My rod choice is a 9½-foot graphite with a detachable fighting butt. Having that butt in your pocket reduces some of the weight that you must swing. Never worry about the strength of a rod, as these days those fears are gone. Your body is what needs the care. Gorilla fly rods will hurt you more than any pool-cue surf rod, because we swing fly rods with one arm. Avoid the ultraheavy stuff used by tarpon fly fishermen. You will know more about what I mean when you get to your fourth hour of fishing.

LEADERS AND BACKING

Three things have to be taken into account when we set up strength for the fight: leader, line, and backing. If you are after a fly-fishing world record, you must limit the leader to no more than 20 pounds. I hasten to add that large stripers will demand a 20-pound tippet section. I make my own tapered leaders, because you cannot buy what is needed for big-game fly fishing. Mine are joined sections of 40-, 30-, and 20-pound—3 foot, 2 foot, 3 foot. The last section will shorten up fast from changing flies. You don't need a long leader, and 7 or 8 feet of leader will help in controlling the weight of the hook. You have no control over the strength of the fly line, but I have never had one fail and suspect that most heavy ones are around 25-pound test. Examining the above figures, you'll see that you are going to need a noncorrosive braid that is much stronger than either line or leader. And because of corrosion the margin of extra strength should be substantial, say 40- or 50-pound test. This backing material should be either Dacron or a formulation of Teflon and Dacron; avoid nylon braid, because it is overly large and somewhat corrosive. Remember, if the margin of strength between the leader and backing is too slight, you risk the same kind of loss that I experienced above in the second fish. We do not lament losing expensive fly lines here. We mourn, rather, the end of a night of fly fishing.

SHOOTING HEADS

By definition, a shooting head is a short section of weight-forward fly line, usually 30 feet long; instead of a running fly line, it has a long section of monofilament. Naturally, the mono is lighter than the running fly line, thus lifting more easily because it is lighter and running through the guides more easily because there is less friction. The advantage in the shooting head is simply longer casts with less effort.

How long? Well, an experienced flycaster either standing on dry shore or in a boat, where his stripping isn't being held by water, can deliver 100 feet plus all day with only one false cast. Even under more natural fishing conditions in which the caster lacks a clean place for stripping, he is bound to add 50 percent to his normal length.

Admittedly, all this sounds simplistic. There has to be some reason why more flycasters don't use shooting heads. Distance isn't all that important when fly fishing; fact is, in most situations gamefish will come to the fly inside of 30 feet. If that is the kind of fly fishing you are involved in, you need not read another word. But we talk distance here because it is needed to add a measure of versatility.

Still, you see very few people using shooting heads, probably for a combination of reasons. For one thing, the technique is contrary to tradition in this part of the country, and new things—if we can call heads new—are slow to take hold. Shooting heads act differently than conventional weight-forward fly lines because they are faster in the back cast, causing a slight change in timing. Many feel that they do not handle as well in the wind. My opinion is that a severe wind will, at worse, reduce your cast to what you would get with a regular line. Another understandable objection with which I sympathize is the bump between fly line and mono during the retrieve. This can be particularly unnerving at night when you don't see the fly line approach the first guide. An on-edge or over-ready angler often perceives this bump as a take. And the mono running line is more likely to tangle than fly line. Some casters find 30 feet to be a little more line than they want in the air. It is a fact of fishing with heads that you are not going to do a whole lot until the splice is clear of the tip. The above shortcomings are the necessary trade-offs, as in so many other things, one makes for those 100-foot casts. If you like shooting heads, you could shorten the head by taking 4 to 6 feet off the bottom, and an epoxy splice makes the connection a little smoother, though I don't use one.

While distance should be the primary objective of those who use shooting heads, there are other advantages, however incidental. Sinking lines tend to go down a little faster because of the low resistance in the mono. It appears to be about one line rating in sink rate. That is, a fast sink will probably cover the water that an extra-fast sink would. A fly reel's capacity increases enormously once you go to a shooting head. The reason is that you are removing 90 feet of running fly line, which is fat, and replacing it with 150 feet of mono running line, something that has virtually no impact upon the reel's capacity. If you are anything like I am, and experience tells me you probably are, you are always trying to jam an extra 10 yards into the fly reel to save you from the horror of losing a dream fish to an empty spool. Which brings me to something that I know you are going to do: use mono from your spinning reel for running line. *Don't.* The industry has a special mono for shooting-head use that is formulated not to kink, to lack memory. One of these is called "Amnesia," because it lacks memory (a neat name). Cortland Cobra flat will not coil and curl like regular spin-fishing mono; I've also used Plion running line with good results. An important thing about running lines is that it helps to have them in a bright, fluorescent color so that they are easier to pick up after the cast for stripping those few times you might be fishing in daylight. Bright lines are not going to scare a fish when they are 40 feet from the fly.

Naturally, 150 feet of running line, which can act as backing to some degree, is not going to be enough; this should be added to whatever backing you would normally have on the reel. Moreover, the braid will cushion the tendency that mono has to expand and apply forces upon the reel's spool.

Yes, I thump for the shooting head, but as much as they have done for me in distance casting, I think you ought to know that I have friends who don't like them. Any serious fly caster should try one, because it isn't like going out and buying a whole new outfit. The cost of a shooting head, often called a shooting taper, is about half what a full fly line of the same size would be. A spool of running mono is $3.00. If it works out for you, you'll cast like Ted Williams. It's a pretty neat feeling to see guys false casting their brains out to get enough line into the air—and no fly swishing in the air ever caught a fish—and then you effortlessly dump your offer way past anybody else, nobody knowing why.

According to books, shooting heads originated in the west for steelhead fishing around 1950. Were I privileged to make an addition to what they say, I would add that New Englanders have been slow to accept them, failing to recognize the advantages in big-water fly fishing.

RIFFLE HITCH

The riffle hitch should be included in that bag of tricks that all fly fishermen keep stored in their mind. Sooner or later you are going to be confronted with an angling situation in which this method, like fishing deep or drifting dry on the top, will help to make fish take.

Riffling, tying off your fly so that it drags on the top, has been done by Atlantic salmon fishermen for one hundred years—admittedly nothing new. What amazes me is that I have never heard of other angling types putting it to work. I never would have thought of it myself were it not for my own salmon-fishing experiences. Here, as you might expect, I've often found that salmon will lie in a pool, seemingly sullen and disinterested, until the fly *drags* over their heads on the surface. Then, as if compelled by some deep inner hatred for anything that would dare move past their lie with such abandon, they will go about killing it with the kind of resignation that has made the species famous. In every case where the riffle hitch came through for me, it was after wet flies, attached in a more traditional manner, had been tried; in at least half the instances, dry flies had been used with no positive results. Much as we wish we could, we lay no claim to originating the technique; it's one of those old-as-the-hills things you can find in any salmon-fishing book.

As far as I know, the "hitch" got moved from salmon fishing for the first time about five years ago, when I came home from Quebec. I was surfcasting for stripers with the fly rod on Cape Cod at night and catching a few school fish, 4 to 8 pounds, but not satisfied with my results. It seemed to me there were far more striped bass in the surf than the action I was having would indicate. With salmon fishing so fresh in my mind, it occurred to me to try to riffle to see if it would boost the number of hits I was getting.

Typically, the linesides were feeding upon sand eels and sperling, two species of bait fish that show a pronounced tendency to disturb the surface even when unmolested. I have often found them with my flashlight just lying at rest on the top, their noses breaking the surface tension. With predators cruising the shallows, one can easily envision what escaping bait, and their resultant commotion, might do to the surface.

With my fly tied off so that it would create a small motion line—a V-wake that sent out the message, "Here I am, here I am"—it stood to reason that my fly was going to be more evident to any potential taker. In this particular application it is a case of getting their attention, making the fly more evident, as well as simulating the behavior of the bait fish itself. Admittedly, the first night I tried it there were plenty of stripers around. After an hour of fishing the usual way, I was convinced that I lured more hits with the riffle. In the subdued quarter moonlight, I could see the "little duck," as my wife likes to call it, swimming in the current, the bass rising behind it and gulping without the slightest hesitation. From then on I rarely fly fished for stripers without using this method.

What makes the hitch a notable technique here is that it gets their attention through a more subtle breaking of the surface. True, you can bring attention to a fly by using a splashy, floating, popping bug that splats along on the surface with apparent abandon, sometimes with favorable results, but the hitch is more in keeping with the mistakes that other forage in the wild might make. It is more a sleight of hand.

To tie the riffle hitch, use any knot that you would normally use to attach the fly to leader. Then wind a simple overhand knot in the leader a couple of inches above the fly, leaving it loose in a loop. Holding the head of the fly up, tighten the overhand loop around the neck of the fly so that the leader leaves the fly from the side at the thread windings. Repeat the overhand knot in the same way so that two overhands are tight at the fly's neck. This is necessary to keep the first overhand from loosening. Keep in mind that any overhand knot that is allowed to close upon itself on the leader will reduce the strength of your leader by half; such knots are self-destructive. But if the knots are closed around the neck of a fly, the fly keeps the leader from cutting into itself, and there is no reduction in strength. It is a good idea to have the leader leaving the fly toward your bank when the fly faces upstream; salmon fishermen prefer it this way, and they are the ones, after all, who champion the method. I have fished the opposite bank of a river without retying it, however, and found that there was no change in the performance of the fly. Certainly, putting a half twist in 8 to 12 feet of leader is something that currents against the fly can do with little effort.

Though having the leader come off the fly from the side seems unnatural, that's what makes the fly plane on the top. The principle, if not the same, is similar to that of a side-planer used in trolling. Here, however, it is often the water that is moving as well as the fly. We would be remiss if we failed to emphasize that the hitch must be used in fast-moving water: rivers or strong tiderips. Where currents tend to be too weak to push the fly to the surface, it may be necessary to increase the speed of the retrieve, but I dislike having to resort to that. Still, as I am sure most experienced anglers know, strange things can work at times, and trying is what it is all about. I'm convinced, too, that the riffle hitch shows its best side for a striped bass at night. There are things that you can do to help the fly along as a surface tempter. Smaller hooks with lighter, wispier dressings or more naturally floating materials like bucktail permit the fly to ride higher. We hasten to add, though, that that can be overdone, because this is not a dry fly, and a fly that is riding too high may undermine the subtle effect you are trying to achieve. As a starting point you might want to ride higher in the dark, but in the daytime only leave a line on the surface.

I know I'll never again face a fly-fishing situation where gamefish are in evidence without tying off my fly so as to make it ride the riffles and hydros like a little critter fighting the current in order to tempt a bruiser from below.

CONDITIONS

You don't want to fly fish in a heavy sea from the beach. A good rule of thumb is that if you can't cast a light plug, maybe the fly rod needs a rest. No doubt some imaginary distance requirement holds a lot of people back from fly fishing the beach, but surfcasters have an advantage in that the wash is a feeding place for both stripers and bluefish. If you can reach that wash, then, distance may be less of a factor in sea fishing than many of the traditional applications of the fly rod. I know you want numbers, and 40 to 60 feet comes to mind, but I wouldn't want to clean all the stripers I've caught at 15.

Much of our striper fishing is estuarine or protected in some way. Bays, tidal rivers, shoreline inlets—particularly inside or in the back—have no pushy surf to tangle fly lines. On flat dull nights when the suds are gentle, the bass are picky and hard to take, and this is when they come more readily for that fly than anything else.

Dealing with marginal nights has to be an individual decision. Competent fly fishermen are usually undaunted by wind. All outdoors people, with any time in grade, long ago learned that the elements go with the sport, so one person's limit might be nothing more than a casual inconvenience to another. Typically, after a few yards of retrieve, there is stripping or retrieved fly line that has to be dealt with. Never coil this tightly in your hand the way old-time trout fishermen used to. It is not good for the line coating, it can tangle on your fingers, ruining your night, or the slightest fouling can catch in the guides and rip one off just before the leader breaks. My choice is to let it fall into the surf, though water movement can be inconvenient. Some surf fly fishermen, according to books, use a stripping basket to lay the fly line for the prevention of fouling and surf interference. I hate the baskets and want nothing around my front where I am holding a rod during the set and fight.

Saltwater fly fishing is fraught with gimmickry. Many so-called "pros" boast of numerous big-game conquests through fly fishing. Many, but not all, have made their mark by luring great fish to the surface, skipping a hookless bait behind the boat, or have worked a well-cast plug to within fly-casting range with gamefish panting when the fly hit the water. Others have simply gone to fly fishing for the excitement of "light tackle," and I have even known others, using "fly rods," who drifted bait to stripers. Much of this has done little but give true fly fishing a bad name as stunt fishing. Indeed, such methods with less than sensible intent should be put to rest for one simple reason: Fly fishing is an incredibly effective method for taking bass.

⪦ *Wading Equipment* ⪧

C ontrary to widespread custom, there is a variety of
garments that can be utilized to keep you dry while
providing good mobility and safety. Ordinary boot-
foot waders will probably remain the mainstay of surfcasters,
but there are a number of options serving our needs that both
reflect the changing designs in surfwear and better address
mobility and safety.

For example, hip boots and oilskin pants, while about the
same in weight as boot-foot waders, provide a little more mobility. Application of this set of garments is particularly ad-
vantageous while fishing rockbound shores and jetties where
there is no true wading. Such rocky shorelines tend to expose
the angler to greater amounts of splash than green water.
Here it is a case of protecting the legs when an occasional
wave breaks or when landing a fish. The hippers provide limited wading potential, and the oilskin pants give splash protection. Where sandy beaches drop off quickly, the hippers
will serve the caster well, but when you need to wade out to a
bar, or in estuarine situations, hippers are limiting. Hip boots
tend to last longer than waders, and the oilskin pants are usually already a part of most anglers' wardrobes.

STOCKING-FOOT WADERS

By definition, stocking-foot waders enclose the fisherman in a watertight garment, but within themselves they provide no footwear, so a wading shoe, which is designed to be exposed to the rigors of water, is necessary. Advantages are that the fabric tends to be extremely lightweight, and shoe design provides superior ankle and foot support. All wading shoes that I've ever used have had felt soles, which enhanced mobility on slippery rocks way beyond that available with other footwear. I'm convinced that you could play basketball in such an arrangement. Moreover, because of the separate nature of wader and shoe, it is possible to wear out several pair of stocking-foot waders while retaining the same wading shoes. This setup is perfect for use on rocky shores and estuarine situations.

The disadvantage of stockingfoots is in beach use, where sand and gravel tend to work in between the shoe and wader. Depending upon the amount of sand intrusion, there can be added weight, damage to the wader's water integrity, and outright discomfort, so it is necessary to seal out this sand. This can be done through a number of options, depending on the design: Old socks between shoe and wader will displace sand for up to two hours, but the sand has to be emptied periodically. Gravel cuffs designed for this work well if the fit is right. Neoprene waders equipped with a built-in gravel guard will seal out sand for up to four hours.

Neoprene stockingfoots, while costing up to three times that of fabric ones, last longer, provide more warmth, patch more easily, and offer the greatest level of buoyancy of any of the options discussed thus far. But the incessant sand intrusion is a disadvantage that must be weighed closely against the mobility and comfort offered by stockingfoots.

At Montauk a small cult of surfmen have been wearing wet suits in surfcasting for a number of years now. I presume the advantage is an ability to swim to otherwise inaccessible bars or leave them when the tide makes conventional wading im-

Surfcasting can be a dangerous activity. Listen to your fears.

possible. No doubt there is added warmth, enhanced flotation, and resilience to the effects of water. But never having used a wet suit in surfcasting, I am not equipped to elaborate further.

The angler who utilizes all types of waders, probably in some cases from other types of fishing, can determine through trial and error which footwear he or she wants to use for a given situation. Surfcasters who want but one pair of waders for all applications would be best equipped with a conventional boot-foot wader.

WADER BELTS

Use of a web belt to cinch in waders around the waist, or complete the closure between parka and wader in particularly wet situations is necessary. Even on quiet nights when a gentle surf is running and the parka (oilskin top) isn't necessary, the belt acts as a closure to keep the surfcaster from taking on heavy quantities of water. There are clearly some situations in which a wave could pour in above the water line, where no outside water pressure were pressing the wader against the body to keep it out, so the surfcaster would be containerizing water in the waders. At 62 pounds per cubic foot, he or she could suddenly become too heavy to be able to manage, unable to exit the surf. Other situations, say where you suddenly find yourself in deep water entering feet first, which is most likely, water pressure would wring the space between wader and body.

It is thus dangerous to say that a belt will always save you from drowning in all situations, but it is equally dangerous to discard the "safety belt" as ineffective. The complexities and individual differences (water, anatomy, type of entry) of each situation prevent us from making a solid statement on the belt's effectiveness as a safety device.

Advantages of the belt that contain no controversy are that it distributes the weight of waders more evenly by sharing that weight between the waist and shoulders, much in the way that a backpack does, and a belt cinched around the waist creates a pocket that can be utilized for carrying gear and personal items.

PART THREE

METHODS—
BAIT AND ARTIFICIALS

∾ *Live Bait* ∾

Many of the largest stripers ever taken, along with most of those of any size that I've seen, fell for live bait. Perhaps the reason for this is that everything else either imitates forage species or lies so quietly on the bottom that predatory stripers fail to notice it. With live bait, if it is part of the striper's diet, chances are very good that any bass in the vicinity is going to take it. The rest is up to you. We limit the discussion here to free-swimming fishes, that is, mackerel, pogies, alewives, shad, and, of course, the live eel.

Before much more is said, I emphasize that the latter, the live eel, is the most important and effective choice of surfcasters anywhere on the Striper Coast; indeed, the eel is so important that few bait and tackle shops fail to carry it. They know that there is a demand, and those who use them know that when they cast a live eel they have a silent partner working out there for them 100 percent of the time. Why are eels such unmitigated murder in the striper surf? They are effectively trapped by bait gatherers; they are comfortably kept in tanks and transported; once sold, the angler can easily get them to the shore, keeping them alive for as long as might be needed to get through a night of fishing. Most of all, bass take them with abandon.

This fact is so commonly accepted by knowing striper anglers everywhere that it has given rise to an interesting theory about the relationship between eels and stripers. It might be half truth and half folklore, but airing of it here may lend a greater understanding of the relationship that the eel enjoys with linesides. The striper is an anadromous fish, that is, it spawns in freshwater rivers. Conversely, the eel (*anguila rostrada*) is catadromous, a freshwater fish that spawns in saltwater. Inasmuch as both must use the rivers to gain access to their respective spawning, it is easy to view them as going in opposing directions, sharing a common environment at a critical time. Consequently, each species is thoroughly aware of the other. The theory, so often spoken by surfcasters, is that the eel is the striper's arch enemy, some say through competition, others say because of predation in both directions, particularly while trailing bass in the spawning grounds. So many things said by striper anglers are unfounded that when I first heard this, I dismissed it as another of those mood stories that surfcasters so often tell late in the night to relieve the boredom.

Then, years later while fishing for a species not unlike bass in Maine, because salmon too are anadromous, we watched the salmon leaping violently clear of the river's surface. And as we sat on the bench awaiting our turn to cast for them, the theories as to why these ocean fish jumped so were aired. Some said that the salmon were like athletes, working out to prepare themselves for the upriver trek to spawning grounds. Others reasoned that the silver sea-runs were feeling the falls and taking to the air to view their next obstacle. I had heard these things before, perhaps because we had read the same books. Then one fellow offered a possible reason that was both fresh and interesting. He said that the salmon were trying to escape the eels, which sought to penetrate their gill covers. His logic was that the eel was trying to "bleed" the salmon so as to feed off its carcass upon its expiration. I sloughed off the theory until a couple of years later, when a Massachusetts salmon biologist complained bitterly to me of the loss of a pair of salmon that they had failed to remove from their return trap promptly—eels had killed them by tearing open their gills.

Arch enemy, or delicacy, it is of little importance whether stripers hate or love the eels. They take them, and the reason is moot.

Avoid still fishing an eel on the bottom with a sinker. Some surfcasters fish eels this way, but a complicated rig attached to a fresh bait will often come back hopelessly balled to the point where neither rig nor bait can be saved. True, their feisty nature can be reduced by slapping them on a rock or the bumper of a beach-buggy, but then you don't have a *live* eel any more. Fished properly, the eel is a free-swimming live bait. Well-selected eels will cast nicely without any outside help, and they will drift about in current or wiggle while retrieved. We say "selected," because having a bucket full of eels that run a range of sizes from 10 inches to 22, which are eating size at Christmas time in New York, will give you fits because of their variability in weight. A 15-inch, 3-ounce bait is the perfect size for both spinning- and conventional-reel fishing. While we mention these specifics as important, the wise surfcaster makes requests softly at the bait shop, because the industry would be in an awful mess if everybody were demanding the same size bait. Moreover, many shops in which I've bought the baits were tended by the proprietor's wife, who was a little jumpy handling the things any more than she had to; overdemanding buyers often got a wrinkled finger pointed at the door or the heavens themselves. Which brings us to a common fear.

Eels, sometimes called "snakes" by the old-guard surfmen I've known, do painfully resemble their informal namesake. Many grown men fear the things enough to fish some other way even when the gang is blitzing 40-pounders to the exclusion of all other methods. Other than a vague similarity in shape, eels are incapable of inflicting any harm upon humans, because there are no teeth or venom. Years ago when I was a budding surfcaster who ritualistically ended each night of fishing by disrobing and rinsing in the surf, I used to fish the night with them in my shirt. Always they found a quiet spot, a tuck above the belt, and lay quietly until it was time to fish.

Eels need to be hooked in a way that will allow them to withstand the forces of casting. Through the mouth and out the bottom is generally effective.

They kept that way for hours, because eels breathe nicely out of the water. They must either have water with fresh air in it, constantly replenished, or they must be kept cool and allowed to breathe open air. Never put them in a bucket of water, because they will deplete the oxygen and suffocate. They can also drown in their own slime. But if placed in a canvas bag, preferably moist with a few ice pick–size punctures, they are restrained, cool, and able to breathe. I've used two excellent types of bags: money bags, which are used for cash deposits at banks, and the canvas bags used as containers for lead shot. Anybody who reloads shotgun shells can give you all of these that you need. When the bag is tucked under your surf belt, none of the baits can escape.

Keep the rig for fishing eels live simple. Tie mono line to a barrel or swivel, and have no less than 30 inches of heavier mono—30 pound for those fishing a 20-pound casting line—tied to a 6/0 or 7/0 hook for a leader. I've never fussed over exact hook style, but do make it a point to avoid long shanks and those with bait holders. Some have up to two bait-holder slashes, which can stick a palate and cause a taker to drop it. Long shanks are simply extra unneeded steel that might alarm them. My favorite hook style, which has demonstrated effective qualities, is a Mustad 92625. No factory hook is sharp enough to be used without first improving it with a mill smooth file. We require long mono leaders, because if you look down the throat of a 50-pounder—something anyone who reads this is bound to do (just kidding)—you will see that 24 inches is needed just to cover the distance from gullet to the lips, and you don't want the barrel touching those lips. Similarly, you will fool few stripers while using a wire leader.

When baiting up insert the hook point in the mouth, down the throat roughly an inch, and out the bottom. An arrangement such as this will maximize the bait's life—commonly up to an hour—and still provide enough material to withstand the rigors of casting. I know that you will hear of a method of inserting the hook through both lips, but that is done by boatmen who never have to concern themselves with serious casting and the forces involved. As long as your bait presents a slight bend in the tail when held out of the water, it is lively enough to use.

Once an eel is on the hook, it tends to ball up on the leader, writhing until it has tightened the mono around its own throat in a sort of *hari-kari*. When this happens the best advice is to cut the whole thing apart and start again. In order to prevent this, it is imperative that you do not bait up until the moment you are ready to fish. As soon as the eel is hooked, hold onto the body with a slight tension against the tip, and get off a rapid swing of a cast for any distance. This is usually enough to calm the thing down, and it is a certainty that your third cast will be trouble free.

One of the things that makes eel fishing a perfect medium is that it lacks the boredom of bait fishing the bottom while approaching the stand-on-your-feet nature of plug fishing. The wise eel fisherman "plugs" an eel with a retrieve speed of roughly one third to one half that of a swimming plug, after allowing a few seconds for it to reach the bottom. Eels sink, so casters who like working a beach, rather than waiting for a fish to come along, enjoy the best of both worlds: plugging and bait fishing. We hasten to add in our enthusiasm that operating depth can be modified by starting the retrieve sooner and accelerating the retrieve for a higher ride; moreover, nights or places where the surf is weedy, that single hook bait will come in a lot cleaner than any other possible bait or lure that you could use.

I was going to say a great deal about the take, that moment when you will love me and the eel. Some takes are a subtle tightening of the line, others are violent shots that reflect a greater speed. Either way you cannot come back quickly or you risk a weak penetration at the mouth. Surfcasters have spent many hours debating just how much time should be allowed for the lineside to move off with the eel. Commonly related to a count of ten, some say 50 feet is far enough for the bass to have the eel all the way down; if it is, there is no way that you are going to drop the fish. The hazard in that method, however, is that sometimes a bass will either feel the hook or the resistance of the line and spit it out. Others say that a strike as soon as the take is felt assures that the fish has had no time to drop it. The debate rages. I have often thought that Rhode Island surfcasters like to allow the ten-count, and Cape Codders are the fast hitters. Neither group bats 1.000. For years we eeled the Rhody shore using the ten-count and had few fish drop the bait.

Another complexity that should be addressed here is preventing a tight line between the take and the set. Surfcasters who use spinning, which is most, would best retrieve with an upright rod. Because it is difficult to open a bail that is under the tension of tight line—and it can tighten mighty fast—the rod tip can be dropped seaward, throwing as much as 12 to 15 feet of slack for the run. The angler then steps forward, opening his bail along the way. Whatever the take time might be, it is decided by the angler and not by the violence of a prematurely tight line. It can deplete your sense of control when you've decided to fish the Rhode Island way—letting them run—and then catch most of your stripers Cape style, by striking fast.

Those who fish conventional or revolving-spool equipment enjoy a quicker response, because they need only step forward and throw a clutch, thumbing the line softly as it tumbles from the spool. Of course, if the bass moves off in a huff and the line backlashes during that run, you are going to lose. It sounds painfully complicated, but I have messed the whole thing up many times and still caught the lineside in spite of myself.

Impose no restrictions on live-eel fishing that you don't see here. Here is some of the folklore that I've heard over the years: Eels don't work in the spring; you can't tell when you have a hit in rough water; they don't work in a particular area.

An eel will work as long as there are stripers in the area, be it spring or some place where eels are not sold. At times, while fishing Outer Cape Cod, eels were difficult to get. When this happened, and it happened because there was little local demand, we brought them in from Buzzards Bay or Rhody and murdered stripers.

RIGGED EELS

When a bait is dead, but not lying immobile on the bottom the way a dead bait is usually presented, and, worse, is "plugged" as though it were an artificial, how should we be talking about this bait? The problem here is that the rigged eel is a little of all of these things: It is dead, yet does not ap-

Rigged eels can be murder on big stripers, and they are more efficient for covering the water than live ones. They are usually fished more like a lure than a bait.

pear to be so, and, in a sense, is much like an artificial because of the way it is fished. The rigged eel also is delightfully castable and most effective.

One thing peculiar to this bait is the fact that all the surf-casters I know who wouldn't dream of going out on the beach without them are died-in-the-wool plug fishermen. Bait or lure, the eel, in this case, is cast and retrieved as though it were an artificial. Of course the uninitiated always ask why it is necessary to use a genuine eel for this application. The feeling is that the same thing can be accomplished with a rubber or plastic molded version of an eel, but that is not the case. As yet no formulation of plastic or rubber has come about with the suppleness required to match a true eel. In addition, there are other advantages that rigged eels have even over live ones.

Many surfcasters feel that a rigged eel is superior to a live one. We certainly don't have to worry about keeping them alive, for one thing. Because of the weight and style of the hooks, they cast better than live eels and sink more quickly, thus offering depth of fishing options that are accomplished more efficiently. In addition, since a rigged eel is plugged, it is possible to cover twice the water with a rigged eel than with a live one and certainly as much beach as one is capable of covering with any plug or lure. Lastly, no striped bass on this planet is going to straighten this hook type as they often do with plugs, which are cursed by a variety of accidental fulcrums.

In the previous section (pages 127–33), when we talked about selecting live eels, I emphasized that it is often necessary to purchase eels of similar size in order to deal with casting requirements, but I pointed out that some compromise is necessary because eels do not all come in the same size. But where rigging is concerned, the particular bait is going to spend twenty to fifty times—assuming no encounters with bluefish— the amount of time on the end of your line that a live one does. I would be much more concerned, consequently, with uniformity of size when choosing rigged eels. You might even want to have two sizes in use: one for spinning and another for conventional. For conventional and heavy spinning, a 15- or 16-inch eel is a good size. Never worry about ole bucket mouth's ability to take such a size.

Never rig an eel that is still alive. Along with being unnecessarily gruesome, it is more difficult and inconvenient. Anyone who has fished live eels will know that they die quickly in too little water. Overly complicated techniques designed to kill the eel without damaging the body—like electrocution— have been written about from time to time in the magazines and are patently stupid, because they are dangerous and unnecessary. Naturally, the eel is going to be stiff from *rigor mortis*, but this can be plied out by vigorous wiping with a paper towel, which is being used to remove the coating of slime that the bait is going to have.

For an overview of what is to be accomplished, two 9/0 Siwash salmon hooks, sharpened to a needle, have to be placed with their shanks inside the body, with the bends and points protruding below at center so as to have a keel effect upon the bait. (Mustad hook style 9510X3T or 9510X3S.) A section of leader must travel within the body from the rear hook, which protrudes at the eel's vent, to the front hook. Once the two hooks are in place, the rear one must be secured at three points: from each side of the eel's body through the hook eye and at the bend. The forward hook has the eel's mouth wrapped down tight just below the hook's eye and lashed at the bend. Keep in mind when rigging: A rigged eel is not a bait that is used once and then thrown out. It can be fished, stowed, frozen, thawed, and fished again and again; it also must be able to withstand the rigors of casting and retrieving for many hours, along with the forces of, with luck, many fine striped bass.

The type of leader that is used to run from the rear hook forward varies with individual riggers. I have seen 50-pound braided line used for this, along with heavier sections of mono. Because of the corrosive nature of these materials, I have always used crimped, nylon-coated 60-pound wire. I keep a variety of lengths in my kit, matching them up with individual baits. You need two kinds of rigging needles, which can be fashioned from a metal coat hanger: a 9- or 10-inch needle for the body length and a 2- or 3-inch one for sewing the hooks in place. The coat-hanger steel can be easily forged flat with a hammer at one end, then drilled, a hole roughly $\frac{1}{16}$ inch, for attaching line. The opposite end should be sharpened. Use old braided line for threading the wire leader forward and for sewing the hooks into position.

After selecting a rear hook with a leader of the proper length, tie some braid to the forward loop of the leader, then tie the other end to the eye of the longer rigging needle. Run the needle from the eel's vent up through the body and out the mouth. If your planning is right, the loop on the wire leader should come out just outside the eel's mouth. Then run the point of another salmon hook down the throat so as to have it come out underneath at the bend in the hook. Both the eye of the head hook and the loop of the vent hook should be in alignment. At this stage gravity is acting upon the hooks, and they tend to hang haphazardly, so they must be sewn into position in order to stay pointed downward. Using the short needle and a section of the old braid, feel for the large eye of the rear hook, penetrate the body with the needle point, and sew the braid through so as to tie the eye of the hook to one side of the body; repeat this on the opposite side. Then at the place where the bend of the rear hook leaves the body, sew through the meaty portion and tie it in place. When finished, the rear hook will be held in three places, with all Irish pennants trimmed off. The front hook is positioned where it leaves the throat in the same way. Lastly, wrap some braid around the eel's mouth right below the eye of the front hook as tight as you can; it is imperative that this tie off not slip aft when under strain. What I do is run the line through the eye after tying off, then tie it off again. Both hooks should be pointing downward of an upright body when finished and be *securely* in place.

After the eel is rigged, the most important operation is breaking all the vertebrae in the eel's body. This is accomplished by folding it over onto itself and squeezing, first in one sideways direction and then the other. When this is done there will be a light cracking sound very similar to that of knuckles cracking. When done full length, particularly from the vent aft, the bait becomes very supple and all *rigor mortis* has been allayed. It is this operation, introducing suppleness by breaking the vertebrae, that distinguishes true rigged eels from the molded rubber creations. I have often weighed the differences between them and found that no formulation of rubber even comes close to a true eel in flexibility. A simple test is to lay a rubber one down on the edge of a table beside the true article with both their tails hanging over the edge.

You will see that nature's eel rolls off the edge more sharply.

Never attach the rigged eel to your leader with any kind of terminal. The leader should be run through *both* the eye of the front hook and the loop of the rear hook's leader. If you want to see what all the excitement is about with rigged eels, strip 15 feet of line from your reel and toss the bait into the water, moving it toward you with the tip. You will note that the body has almost frantic horizontal undulations, that the thing virtually slithers through the water.

Years ago when the blue Atom swimmer was so popular in the Cape surf, some enterprising surfcaster discovered that if you rubbed an eel with beach sand you could expose the blue color that is in an eel's underbody. I have done this from time to time, resulting in no discernible difference in the effectiveness of the bait. But I hasten to add that any failure to recommend "blue eels" is apt to be viewed with a measure of dismay from many regulars.

It is important to keep rigged eels in an ice chest while fishing. Once you are home they can be frozen indefinitely; in fact, they can be thawed and fished, refrozen, and fished again an unlimited number of times. Some of my baits—and I have always thought enough of them to have many on call—have journeyed in and out of my freezer for up to four years and still produced striped bass. Even those that dried and stiffened on the rod, during a long session of plug fishing, came back to life after being in water a few minutes.

It is not enough to have the finest natural bait known to stripermen. If the rigged eel is not retrieved properly, action imparted to it as it comes, your efforts will either be fruitless or woefully similar to that of a mediocre plug. The standard retrieve speed is about the same as a swimming plug, which is quite slow; to get the most out of the special body qualities of the eel, however, it should be pumped often with jerky and erratic motions. Many surfcasters try to avoid a pattern to these motions, while others maintain a rhythm. We refer to the "standard" retrieve, because from time to time you will find it necessary to make a departure.

When stripers are about, it is not unusual to feel something on the eel that is subtle, almost ghostlike. Incidentally, these whisper feelings are also common while plug fishing but are more difficult to discern. Such sudden motions will cause many casters to haul back, fanning upon the feeling without finding the mark. Though I cannot prove it, I am convinced that these are the result of a striper's body turning away from the offer, because the hydraulic effect of a 30-pound-plus fish moving suddenly that close to the bait disturbs the surrounding water enough to influence a feel upon the line. What is significant here is that the angler is being told that a lineside is nearby and had some interest in the eel, but that, unaccountably, it has rejected it.

When we first had such experiences, Joyce and I were quite surprised to hear that the other had had the same rustling feelings at the end of the line. It proved that we were not imagining it. Slowing the retrieve was fruitless, as it seemed to happen more often; our only option was to speed up. When I tried it I was rewarded with a distinct slam to the eel that struck so hard I didn't need to even haul back in response to the take; moreover, my experimenting wife and companion started taking bass with the high-speed retrieve as well.

This was not one of those fluke situations that never repeats itself. Many times during that first season when we discovered bass were rejecting our baits, we speeded up in response to the symptom. It became such a common occurrence that we dubbed the technique the "100-mile-per-hour retrieve." We had such confidence in what we were doing that we often fished this way with the eel without waiting for indications of its need. Of course, its failing is that fishing this way is hard work. When you consider that the riggy has to be pumped, and now it was going as fast as we could retrieve it, the labor involved is mindful of fishing a popping plug. That's not as pleasant as fishing a lazy swimming plug or a rigged eel in the fashion that we had known and that is widely used. You do what you have to do.

Bluefish love eels. If a surfcaster has a mind to fish for

blues, it is advisable to use live eels. It is not practical to put a rigged eel out there in a sea replete with bluefish teeth. The surfcasters whom I have known, and I am no exception, find the presence of bluefish the bane of rigged-eel fishing. After all, we have applied no small amount of craft to preparation of the bait, and having it destroyed by a bluefish that has vandalized the thing by neatly nipping the tail off is surely the ultimate degradation and a distinct impediment upon our striper fishing efforts. Don't get me wrong: The bluefish is a fine gamefish, and it has saved many midwatch hunts along the beach when we were unable to find bass. But we speak of rigged-eel fishing here, and it cannot be done when, as my dear old surfcasting friend and rigged-eel fisherman George Carlezon used to say when referring to the choppers, "them sons-a-bitches is in the surf."

We've all lost some of our dearly loved baits to bluefish, but my most memorable experience was in the late seventies, just east of Highland Light on the Cape. At the time we had a strong pick of very large bass going nightly with more of them over 40 pounds than under. In more than a week of fishing, we had not seen a solitary bluefish and avoided discussing it out of fear of arousing some obscure surfcasting god.

I was pumping away on my bait, half ready because the fishing had been good, when I felt the sudden pull that separated itself just as the rod bent. I might have thought it a bass for an instant, but the reduced weight of my offer—which was a clear signal that half of it was gone—was apparent; only a bluefish can do that. Others I have known would have rushed the bait out in a vain effort to save it. But knowing that it was futile, I was determined to put an end to the creature that had so degraded my efforts. If he came back I would be ready for him and a much higher percentage of what I had out there was protected with hooks. Fortunately, the strike had come early in the retrieve, providing enough water to continue the effort. Pumping what remained, I tried to make it as tantalizing as I could under the circumstances, but a rigged eel without a tail—and it had to be gone—is like a

Manhattan without bourbon. Then there was a hard pull, and I hauled back, not in a desperate way like a surfcaster who wants to catch a fish, but in the way of somebody who wants to get even. It seemed strange to me that this bluefish was taking so much line. There were none of the throbs and shakes that one can usually associate with a bluefish. My mind was thinking bluefish, though I had not seen the bait, but my hands and shoulders were telling me that I had drawn blood on a serious striped bass.

After beaching it, a lineside that later weighed 51 pounds, I reached into its maw to retrieve my rigged eel and found, as I had thought in the first place, that the tail had been neatly cut off by a bluefish seconds before this fine fish inhaled it.

This was indeed a lucky turn of events for me. It resulted in the taking of one of my largest stripers ever. Maybe that is one of the things about surfcasting that causes so many of us to become incurably bound to the sport. Each night, each tide, the arbitrary choice to fish this way or that, or to cast short, left, or right, introduces another wild card in a game that we cannot wait to play. Yet even without taking such choices into account, the sea abounds with mysteries of its own that remind us all of how frail and limited our knowledge of surf fishing really is.

EEL SKINS

Long before I arrived on the Striper Coast, surfcasters were skinning eels and putting them on swimming plugs. Such "skinplugs" are another excellent utilization of leftover live eels.

To prepare the eel skin, nail the eel at the head end to either a section of driftwood or to the back shed. Make a circular cut through the skin just below where it is nailed, peel back the skin, and pull it off as you would with a sock. This procedure turns the skin inside out, exposing its blue coloration. Then slide the skin over the body of a swimming

An eel skin creates a tantalizing action in swimming plugs.

plug that has had its hooks removed and tie it down at the head, leaving the swimming plate exposed. Make small cuts where the hooks are attached for hook placement, but do not attach a hook at the tail of the plug, as it would interfere with the long, streaming tail. Larger plugs, often equipped with only one remaining hook mount, only have one treble. Never worry about this, as the striper is going to take this offer head first anyway.

Aside from a change in coloration, the skin enhances the lure by virtue of the addition of supple length, which is exaggerated by the built-up swimming action of the plug.

Selection of the proper-size eel to fit your selected swimming plug has to be done with the sizes of both the eel and plug in mind. Most skin plugs are made from larger eels—often those too large for ordinary eel fishing. Taking proportions into account, most skins are shortened from the head end by a straight cut across. In order to achieve the right size and action effect, there should be an amount of skin outboard of the plug at the tail, about equal to or slightly shorter than the plug body. Because of the limitations of such natural materials, difficulties of fitting, and variability of results, skin plugs tend to be highly individualistic. Some are good, others are fantastic.

If you are converted to using such creations, eel skins can be skinned out ahead of time and preserved nicely in a solution of kosher salt, then jarred for that night when you feel something special is needed. You can also tuck one into a pork-rind jar, as it will keep well in the existing solution. If allowed to dry out, the skin will soften up again upon contact with water, but never leave a skin to dry on a plug for more than a couple of days.

FREE SWIMMERS

The enterprising surfcaster uses what live bait is in the area, and that can be just about anything. Once during a Race Point blitz, a fellow called out when a bass he had just landed regurgitated a bait fish that he was certain was a coho salmon. It turned out to be an 8-inch weakfish. Within minutes the little squeteague, as they are called in part of their range, were washing up all over the beach, telling us what had drawn so many big stripers to the surf. Another year in Charlestown, Rhode Island, as well as many times since, I saw bass murdering snapper blues. Anyone with a trout rod and ⅛-ounce Kastmaster could have caught his bait and then cleaned up on the true gamefish.

Some lessons can be drawn from the above examples: Stripers will forage upon any small fish, without regard for the fact that we might consider these hapless little creatures as gamefish, and, when we use what is in the vicinity for bait, we can come no closer to satisfying their needs and current feeding habits. It is a sort of coastal analogy to the shopworn, sweet-water angling adage that one must "match the hatch." When such natural bait-gathering opportunities present themselves, there is, admittedly, a slight loss of flexibility, but the compensations can be higher. The reason is that you must acquire and keep bait before you can begin fishing—a measure often calling for considerable resignation.

In Narragansett, Rhode Island, one year, I found the birds diving off the rocky stretch southwest of the pier and beach area at the end of Hazard Avenue. Surfcasters were fishing in a frenzy with small, one-handed trout rods, which seemed a little strange to me. Yet I could plainly see moby stripers exploding upon the surface. A fellow hauled in a tinker mackerel, gently placing it in a pool of splash water behind him. When I examined the pool, I saw that he had several tinkers swimming about. Of course, while making these observations, I had been casting a popping plug where the action seemed to be, but I couldn't bring anything up. Then, farther down the shore, one of the light-tackle men, whose rod had inexplicably changed, hauled back; the great stick arced from the weight of a bull striper, which I later learned had taken a live tinker mackerel that had been towing a large, red-and-white plastic float. During the time that it took him to land it, the other surfman, whom I had been watching more closely, hooked up in the same way. These fellows knew what they were doing.

A mackerel or snapper blue, or any other free-swimming live bait for that matter, doesn't have the hardiness that you get from an eel. And if you don't cast softly, you may have the precious bait tear free, but all the inconveniences are compensated for by their effectiveness.

Rigging for these live baits is slightly different. If there is enough current to carry the bait seaward, as in an inlet, then it may not be necessary to use a float. Many surfcasters like to use a treble hook, size depending upon how large or small the bait is. One barb is used to pin the hook to the bait, and the other two are reserved for hooking the gamefish that swallows the offer. Of course, we face the same problems of when to hit the taker that we discussed when speaking of live eels.

If you ever come upon a school of menhaden (a.k.a.

Live baits rigged with a treble hook allow exposed hook points for the take.

bunker, pogie), you can foul-hook some for bait with a tin that is equipped with a treble hook. Some surfcasters keep a daisy chain of trebles with a bank sinker just for this purpose. Bunkers tend to school tightly, and it is a simple thing to drag hooks through the school to latch onto a few. Nothing will bring a big striper to the pantry quicker than a bleeding bunker. We hasten to add, however, that acquisition of such natural live baits can be unreliable, which is why surfcasters will buy eels and thus be sure of live bait.

Spring is a lean time for hungry migrating stripers, as it is yet too early for great schools of menhaden to appear, and the season for mackerel is usually a long way off. East of Montauk the first big bass flood north around mid-May. Foraging is poor along the beaches, but the estuaries are teeming with alewives (herring), which began their run in early April. This anadromous species runs until mid-June in just about all the streams that have not been ruined by the Industrial Revolution. Consequently, linesides will slip as far up rivers and bays as they dare by day, then venture into incredibly small coves and shallows under cover of darkness for the herring. Just how big a bass and how far inland would confound the most knowledgeable striper anglers. These great fish do so to feed upon the shadlike, oily bait fish of 7 to 10 inches that are spawning. The early alewives are strong and feisty, but the spent fish dropping down are a pushover for predators. Again it is a case of having the fish off their guard, because they have successfully fed on so many herring that yours is not likely to be suspect. On average I'll let a taker run 75 feet before putting the brakes on. Few, especially the bigger ones, will drop a herring during such a run. Most of us will pin a 4/0 treble through an alewife's mouth, which is the part that goes down first on a take.

Just about any arrangement that allows new water in will keep herring alive. For years I used a box with cutouts that had wire stapled over them. I've seen fellows with an inner tube that had a landing net with the handle cut off, inserted through the center, and tied into position. If the stream where you acquire bait is far from where you fish, it may be necessary to rig some kind of tank with an aerator. Some just put their baits in a washtub and hurry, accepting a small mortality as part of the activity.

There are other complications. Most herring runs are in fresh water, which means a fishing license is needed for gathering bait. Regulations for the taking of herring vary from state to state, in some cases with limits. There are strict regulations against "dip netting" in a fish ladder. Never take more bait than you need, as the resource is too precious. Also beware of partners who get their kicks chasing bait around in brooks during the deep night when more time is needed for fishing. Unaccountably, a stream can be teeming with the things one night, and you might be competing with some other striper angler for only a couple of baits. One season a family of raccoons jumped herring at the same falls as I did, but we competed politely.

Our purpose is covering the bases here, and you don't have to do any part of the fishing we speak of if it sounds too complicated. I've done all these things and know that mid-watch waits on a silent river yield a soothing-to-the-spirit charm of their own. The world sleeps while shore birds rustle in the marsh grass. Lying back, the rods silhouetted against the light of some distant bridge or shore drive, we watch for movement in the lines or the sound of a ratchet yielding to the strain of a passing striper.

BIG BAITS

It is not unusual for striper anglers to use a bait that is too large to be cast. One time in Charlestown, Rhode Island, the stripers were coming in on the beach at sunset to murder hickory shad that used to come in on the shore to murder something else.

I have no knowledge of the size ratio of the shad and their quarry, but I can tell you that the stripers were more than 40 pounds, and the shad were around 4. To us the latter were a little big, even for stripers, but if you think about it, ten to one isn't bad for a fish if you've ever seen 10-inch trout gulp 1-inch fry in a small stream. No doubt the notion of size begins to take on meaning when we start trying to throw the things over the wave tops.

The truth is that you don't throw that kind of stuff, you sort of let it go with the reel in free spool, with the hope that when something takes it you will be able to tell the difference. This is because husky baits are strong enough to feel like a striped bass when first released, particularly if your enthusiasm is working upon your imagination. When exploring the pure physics of big baits and, with luck, bigger mouths, I believe that few realize how far a feeding striper is willing to go.

We would be remiss in this section if we didn't mention the "big bait—big fish" theory: If you fish big baits, you are always going to get a striper commensurate with it. I don't believe in it completely, because I've caught too many big fish with *small offers* (as well as too many small fish with large ones). In my case it has been flies that were 3 or 4 inches long and so slim that, when wet, they were smaller than a pencil. We've also taken some brutes on a lone sea worm, and I know of many moby bass that fell for a sand eel on a hook. The theory is a generalization, and you know how dangerous those are. It is probably appropriate to say, "Big bait—big fish" if that is what happened, because that is what other people have been saying—probably since King Tut wrestled a Nile perch onto the bank for the first time. I've seen a lot of big baits, or I wouldn't have chosen to include this topic in our live-bait discussion.

We used to have a guy on Cape Cod who would travel miles seaward in a 14-footer just to jig for big pollock that went into his live bait well. When he had enough he would motor in on the shore to release them with a hook in their backs. The guy was a good fisherman and had a heck of a reputation for taking in some real brute stripers. Of course, part of the reason was that every bass he caught weighed 4 pounds more than it normally would, because he felt that the little fish the big fish ate was now part of the big fish. If you can't follow that: All 46-pounders weighed 50 after they took one of his baits.

One period when big baits came into vogue was when the menhaden or pogy made a cyclical return around 1970. No doubt a few old-timers remembered how to use them and took advantage. On average these weighed between 1 and 3 pounds and, for the time, were a return to husky offerings. The trouble with bunkers is that they have an awful lot of energy and, even with a hook in their backs, can swim too fast to interest a lazy, aging, overweight striper. (Lordy, those are the ones we like to catch.) Ray Jobin, a regular who fished Rhode Island with demonic success in those days, was the first to show the world how to slow a bunker down. What he did was pin a bunker's mouth shut with an old spark plug inside; this solved the problem of having the thing finning on the surface when the fish were down five fathoms and too disinterested to cold trail and hound so far away from the table. It worked. What he never told anybody was that he later went to making a series of slashes in the pogy's side to sap off its energy so that it was catchable by slacker stripers. There probably were scent advantages in the use of a bleeding bait that appealed to a striper's sense of opportunity. He resorted to that, no doubt, when all the V-8s in the junkyard were without plugs. It was a barbaric thing to do to a bait fish, which someone like you and I would never resort to . . . unless we were serious. It was necessary, because big baits swim faster, often too fast.

If you saw a baseball bat in half, that is about the size of a 3-pound squid. One time off Race Point the stripers were acting like animals on the squid. We threw popping plugs into the action, but it didn't do us a bit of good. Our itty-bitty popping plugs were just too small. It was an event worth seeing just the same, because a frightened squid has a little afterburner that is full of high-octane ink that can cause some pretty mobile spurts of movement, in spite of the fact that it is moving backward. Overt size seemed to be the last thing on their predatory minds as a deterrent. If anything the bigness of the bait fish may have even inspired a higher level of feeding activity because of the better effort-to-energy return.

We picked that earlier ten-to-one ratio right out of the air, readily admitting that it doesn't always hold true. It is not unusual to have 6-pound bass taking frisky 1-pound alewives. These schoolies always look a little strained around the gills, but I doubt that they are gulping something of that size for the first time. The fact is that you will often find a couple of alewives already in their stomachs. Oink, oink.

One time I took a twentyish-size bass in Massachusetts's Westport River, and that fish had a pile of winter flounder in her that looked like a stack of pancakes. A week later the fellow who was fishing with me had the same experience. It would be interesting to know if these bass were culling the right-size baits, or if they simply grabbed what was available. The flatties were all of the same size: 8 inches.

It is a slight digression, but I can't resist talking about one of my favorite plugs here. The Creek Chub Giant Pikie Minnow is 13 inches and weighs 4 ounces. Those figures don't sound as big as they look when the thing is in front of you. On the cast it swings badly because of its bulk and has caused more sore back muscles in surfcasters than any artificial that I know. We are not joking about this. Anyway, you will catch monster stripers with the jointed eel, as it is sometimes called, but the 4-pounders that hit it are always a source of astonishment, because they are not twice the length of the plug. Jokes that the striper is trying to do something else to the plug come up every season.

The fact that such big baits for bass are of interest to anglers is kind of an anthropomorphism. We tend to think in human terms, human eating techniques, where we consume small amounts of what we eat at a time. This is because the digestive process begins with chewing. Many fish, not just stripers, are not so equipped and must swallow their forage whole. And while it is all quite natural, it is still neat to ob-

Inexpensive and readily available, sea worms are a popular and effective striper bait.

serve, as well as bearing some accurate lessons in what we can get away with when selecting baits for stripers.

BOTTOM FISHING

The most widely used striper bait in bottom fishing is the sea worm or clam worm (*nereis virens*). Blood worms (*glycera dibranchiata*) are tougher and will stay on the hook longer but are not marketed commercially. If you dig your own, techniques are the same with either bait.

Because clam worms are also popular for other species, a thriving industry exists in Maine, where they are harvested at low tide. These ugly little creatures are somewhat unpleasant to handle, because of their two sharp "pinchers" protruding from the head. The truth is that they really don't harm you, but most of us view their assault as distasteful.

The first dozen I ever bought cost 30 cents, but the price has since climbed to more than $2.00; a dozen sea worms will not carry you very far into the night. There is a price break when buying a flat or "lug," which is ten dozen, and if you plan more than one night of using the things it is in your best interest to have enough bait. The worm's size varies with how far the tide is out when diggers are gathering them: During new and full moons, when there is the greatest exchange of water, they can be as long as 10 inches with a ½-inch diameter; neap tides produce baits as small as 4 inches, and the price does not change.

Of our bottom-fishing baits, the sea worm is the only one that is truly a live bait. They are kept alive by being packed in weed, which is spread on old newspaper, the entire carton cooled in a refrigerator at more than 40 degrees F. If you have bait left, their life can be extended by mixing in quantities of Buss Bedding and periodically culling out dead ones. On occasion we have caught bass with dead sea worms, but these had not been dead very long and remained firm enough for placement on the hook. Such baits should be viewed as inferior, however. Exercise that option only when there are no others.

In the best condition sea worms are soft and will tear from the hook due to the force of a hard or backlashy cast. It is far better to settle for a little less distance and be sure that something remains on the hook. If fishing is good one large worm is enough to lure a big lineside to the take, or, if baits are running small, use two. In either case it is a good idea to leave a small amount of tail trailing off the hook. During the spring, however, when stripers were migrating without benefit of ample quantities of forage, and back when size limits permitted the taking of small bass (say under 25 inches), we used to do well with a 1-inch piece of worm on a small hook, say 2/0.

Earlier, when I called this a popular bait, I was referring to use by anglers of all species. Only a few nights with the worms can show you that everything in the Atlantic will feed upon them. The greatest nighttime curse of using this bait is skates, which can have you tending rods so much that bass are not likely to have a chance at your offer. When this is the case, it is best to use a small torpedo float to lift the baited hook off the bottom. This measure will drastically reduce contact with skates, but of course will not prevent the occasional interloper from accidentally swimming your leader down and getting it anyway.

More about the float. It is unnatural for a piece of cork to be suspending your worms 18 inches off the ocean floor. One of the nice things about the cork torpedo float is that, with its preload on the leader, it can be slid down to the sinker end of the leader out of the way. I would do this during the day when there are rarely any skates about, or when there are so many bass around feeding that the scavengers are not a problem. The float's other disadvantage is that it does impose some wind resistance to the cast and may, in some cases, repel a lineside that has taken the bait, causing it to eject the hook.

Leaders should be about 10 pounds stronger than the line and 18 to 24 inches long after tying or snelling to a 6/0 bait holder offset hook. You will see that the floats come through with a thread loop at one end. Run the tail end of your leader through this loop, then pull both ends of the loop together, pulling the leader through the torpedo. This will install the torpedo upon your leader. Tie the leader end to a barrel or swivel. Later, when satisfied that your rig works, extra ones can be made up either for when you lose a rig or when things are hot and heavy to save time.

A few more things. Sea worms are not a natural or suitable bluefish bait. There are of course times when bluefish have been known to take them, but that was when there were large numbers of bluefish in the area. When baiting a beach you might want to cover the bluefish possibility, then either use another bait entirely or have different rods using different bait.

Some surfmen I have known—always people who did not use sea worms themselves—have the notion that worms are used only in the catching of school stripers. Nothing could be farther from the truth. The fact is that the size limits of worms for catching stripers lie within the stripers themselves. In the late sixties Tom Parker, of Barrington, Rhode Island, took a 68-pound lineside on Nauset Beach. At the time it was the largest bass ever taken from shore. I have since seen a number of fish over 60 pounds caught this way and once gaffed a 55-pounder for a friend.

FORAGING AND WASHUPS

The Atlantic can be a veritable garden of varied bait fish. Strange species often will wash up at the head of the foam, which, in some cases, we can be at a loss to identify: pogy, butterfish, immature alewives, needlefish, squid, sperling, mullet, and mackerel. You can bet that striped bass are willing to make a meal of any of them. One of the most common of these are sand eels.

We zero in on this particular species because they are both common and extremely effective, and they are known to show up in phenomenal numbers at times. If you want to capitalize on the sand-eel option, it is imperative to know as much as possible about the bait you are using; to know sand eels is to know stripers.

While their slender bodies suggest the appearance of an eel, this forage species is not related to the eels we know in any way. *Ammodytes*, the Latin name, are unique in that they burrow into sandy bottoms at times. They will also "dig in" above the low-water mark to await rescue by a rising tide, and, wriggling about above the water line in the wet sand, they are somewhat amphibious. I've observed that the sand eel is largely nocturnal, frequently disappearing by day, along the beach at least, only to show up on the surface at night, sprinkling the surface, either when disturbed by a wading angler or a sudden burst of light. These olive green bait fish may be found from 2 to 8 inches long either washing up on the shore or dug by anglers seeking them for bait with the help of a sand eel rake. This device is similar to a quahog or shellfish rake, but its tongs are closer together and pointed. The gatherer rakes the bottom, penetrating roughly 6 inches, periodically removing those that are impaled and placing them into a container.

Just how many sand eels are applied to the hook depends upon the size of bait that is running. It is possible to string as many as a dozen upon the bend of a hook, and, when they are at the high end of their size, one or two will lure as big a bass as they come to the take. Naturally, as with any bait that is fished dead, it is important that sand eels be as fresh as possible when used. This means that bait should be kept cool when stored. This bait is sometimes available frozen from bait shops, and, if you have no choice, the frozen article can produce. But we remain advocates of a bait that is as near as possible to the live form. The same rig used for sea worms may be applied to sand eels, but these little fishes enjoy a far greater appeal with bluefish, which will snip a mono leader in a second when taking the bait.

I am not as fond of squid for bait as I am of the aforementioned. True, we could publish a healthy volume of names of

those who have taken moby striped bass with a chunk of squid on the bottom, but I have always felt this to be more the exception than the rule. One reason squid always seems to be outperformed by other baits is that its most widespread use is as frozen squid purchased from bait shops. Again, the bait is not fresh. Worse, many surfcasters I have known are in the habit of taking what remains after a night of sitting in the heat and returning it to their freezer for the next trip. By the time this bait nears its end, the stench is enough to gag a mule. Sometimes, bait-shop squid smells this way the moment it begins to soften. Fish should never smell overly like fish. And you'll notice that the squid sold in markets for table consumption never smells that strong.

It is a pity that the strong smell of squid as bait is so widely known. I have eaten squid—known as *calamari* by the Italian chefs who championed its use—and there is no fish I have known with a more tender texture, exquisite flavor, that is more free of scent. Still, resistance is high to using it as a table food, and I strongly suspect that too many of the resisters, as I once was, recall the scent of bad bait. But we are supposed to be talking about what stripers eat, not their antagonists' table preferences.

Earlier I implied that you could use anything that washed up on the beach as a striper bait. Let common sense rule whether you throw the entire fish out there or a piece of it. "Chunks" or cut bait are as old as the hills. The reasons for cut bait are that a slice of mackerel will cast better, emit scent, stretch your supply, and be less at the whim of the currents. But where substantial quantities of meat are involved, I would change the hook to a treble, impaling the bait on two points and leaving one exposed for hooking; still, all points are capable.

There is widespread belief in a hierarchy of bait forms. Naturally, a live fish is out there pumping madly for you in the sense that it gains attention. If keeping such a bait fish alive is not practical, most anglers will reluctantly resort to fishing a whole fish dead—particularly if they have the advantage of feeding it into the current beneath a bridge or the outflow of an inlet. Lastly, and some have to be dragged kicking and screaming to do this, some surfcasters will cut a bait, preferring the head over any other part.

I had an interesting and productive experience with the notion that heads were better, which opened my mind. One June we knew of a substantial school of big linesides that were feeding at the mouth of the Warren River in Narragansett Bay between Rumstick Point and the bay's eastern shore. What with herring (alewives) running in the upstream tributaries, it was an accurate assumption on our part that bass were there to feed upon them. The logistics of getting live herring that far down river on foot, however, were impossible, because it was a long walk for carrying a tank full of water to keep them alive. Casting from the beach, it was impossible to toss a whole herring any distance, and, once it got there, the river's currents made holding bottom impossible. Worse, it was getting too late in the season for us to have all the bait we needed for a night of bottom fishing. We had no choice but to use chunks.

Unintentional as it was, there was a hierarchy in my mind about the various forms of fishing the herring: At the top was a live bait, a dead herring was a compromise, and cut herring felt like a long shot. Even within the options of cut bait, the tendency to rate the various portions—head, center body, and tail—was quite strong, and my tendency was to think that the head would lure more strikes. I was as wrong about that, however, as I had been about which herring presentation would be most effective. The truth was, if we can call results truth, that stripers would pass in the deep night taking the chunks with abandon. We would fish, two of us, two rods apiece, and suddenly the rods would go down in sequence, betraying the direction of their passage, the action more than we could manage at times. Fish from 15 to more than 40 pounds would hammer the pieces of meat that lay on the bottom.

Because the experiment lacked a control, we will never know if the good fishing was due to the method we used, or if the season and place might even have provided better fishing with a live bait, but our experience was enough to carve the value of cut bait in stone.

The fish-finder rig is a standard method of holding a baited hook on the bottom, and it has satisfied all of my bottom fishing needs. The principle of fish finders is that line is allowed to be paid out without dragging the sinker, but that weight is dragged when line is being brought in.

The idea is to run your fishing line through a nylon sinker slide, then tie it off to a large snap-swivel. The sinker slide is equipped with a safety pin–type device, which can be opened, run through the eye of a sinker, then closed, enabling the angler to change sinkers or remove it for travel. Any number of types of terminal gear could be used for the function of holding the sinker, but the nylon slide is less likely to damage the line through the force of casting.

The actual fishing rig consists of a length of leader with a barrel or swivel at one end, which attaches to the snap-swivel that is the stop for the sinker slide, and the hook at the other. Said differently, the order is sinker-slide, snap-swivel, barrel or swivel, leader, and hook. Naturally, the float for lifting bait off the bottom is optional.

You should not go bait fishing with only one rig, and when rods are dancing from hits is no time to be trying to tie up others. All sorts of fates can befall these rigs: You can cast one off, it can be snipped clean of its hook by a bluefish, or a skate can swallow the hook. Any or all of these things can end your fishing or slow you down at a time when efficiency is mandatory. Fishing with one rig is like hunting with one bullet or shell. Even if your first contact is a prize gamefish that makes you feel pretty good, if the hook is buried, that rod is out of commission. When you consider how easy it is to open a snap-swivel for installing another leader with hook, it is a pity to lose any time, because one contact is often indication that a number of gamefish are passing. It is better to have a baited rig waiting in the bucket, so that when you do slide a fish onto the beach all you have to do is open one snap, change the leader, and cast right back out there.

Unless you are directing your efforts specifically toward bluefish, wire leader is bad for your bait fishing. Using it is going to greatly reduce your opportunities to take stripers. I can only speculate why this is, but it seems that the bass simply feel the metal far more easily than they do mono.

In our waters there are two types of sinkers in use: bank sinkers, which are round and will hold on rocky bottoms; and pyramids, which are used for taking a more secure bite on sandy bottoms. If there are no unusual currents, a 3-ounce sinker will keep 20-pound mono in position, and a 5-ounce sinker will secure 30-pound mono. Surfcasters using conventional or revolving-spool reels will find that 40-pound mono reduces casting distance too severely while upping sinker requirements to 6 and 8 ounces, which are murder to cast. Those fishing 20 or 30 may still have to up their sinker ratings to 5 and 8 ounces, respectively, when the water is big.

Bottom fishing can be slow and, understandably, regulars will often fish two or more rods. If this is done wisely, there is nothing wrong with an extra bait out there tolling in gamefish. To get the most out of a second rod, its bait should be placed differently than the other. Incidentally, never overlook that ocean edge in your foreground, which is at the bottom of the slant in the beach, where a foraging gamefish is going to be swimming the length of the shore. There may not be anything wrong with having a bait way out there, but don't make the universal error of thinking that the farther a cast, the more likely a contact. No such rule has even been in place. We hasten to add that it is not where the rods are standing that is important, but where the baits are lying. Spacing your rods along the beach so that all are a long run only increases the chance that you will not get to them on time—and they are more difficult to watch.

It is of course not outside the bounds of probability that a school of fish, any species, might pass and take all your baits at once. If and when this occurs you had better have a sand spike that is both well designed and well buried, or you could end up losing a rod and reel. The question of whether a spike is suitable also relates to how tight a reel's drag is set. Inexpensive lightweight tubes, which are cut on a bias and are easily driven into the sand, can be used as rod holders for baiting up. Their failing is that in order to hold they have to be buried deep, which reduces the length of rod butt within the tube; thus, a well-set tube is not a suitable holder, and, if it encompasses enough of the rod butt, it has not been placed deep enough to prevent it from being pulled over. If you are a one-rod angler who stays with the stick, and you don't go digging in your bag for a sandwich, such tubes will do.

Serious bottom fishermen, however, would do well to have a suitable tube that is attached to a 3-foot length of sharpened angle iron. The angle iron is buried deep without compromising the holding qualities of the tube.

I have seen so many rods claimed by a passing fish, because of poor sand spikes, shoddy installations, or both. One time a guy beside us on Nauset Beach christened a brand-new outfit by having it unaccountably disappear ten minutes after its first cast. He found it so uncanny that the thing could disappear in broad daylight, when his back had been turned for less than a minute, that he was certain—and quite outraged—that one of the gang had taken it as a joke. None of us had seen anything. We found his stick four hours later at low tide with a 4-pound school striper still bouncing in the suds on the end of it. Another time one of the boys went into his camper with his wife during a stretch of time when nobody had caught anything. Two hours later he had a 27-pound bass high and dry on the sandbar in front of his buggy. His rod and sand spike were intact, perhaps because he had learned how to compensate for his habits. Still others, and somehow we hear less about these guys, have had rods disappear mysteriously and never did see them again. These things happen.

In the world of fishing, when somebody is catching a lot of fish, it is usually because that person is doing something right or more right than anyone else. Still, there is a luck of the draw that must also be given some consideration. So often I have seen the fellow on the left hook a fish, then the fellow on the right hook one, and I thought, *"What the hell is the matter with me?"* But I long ago learned to resist the temptation of checking my bait, because I have seen too many others checking theirs when a school of fish was going by. It is one thing to be short that ill-defined edge that someone else is enjoying, and it is another to be unlucky, but it is stupid to have a bait in the water for hours and then remove it when fish are being beached on all sides of you.

Taking a Bait

How do stripers and blues take a bait? The answer to that question is complex. I see no particular pattern that would permit us to guess what has taken a bait by the strike. The reason is that both often exhibit variable striking modes. Bluefish, however, seem more likely to haul a spiked rod down hard, as though it were a trolling rod towing at high speed. This may relate to their seemingly impulsive movements and their tendency to school and forage collectively, so that they are always in competition. Stripers avoid all generalizations.

First, one can never ascertain with any degree of accuracy the size of the bass by the screech of the reel at the take. Conversely, monster fish will often nibble at a bait, jiggling and tugging, as though it were a cunner polishing a hook. Then at other times such brutes might haul a surf rod down so hard that a poorly adjusted drag spelled curtains for the line. We cannot know if this is related to other competing bass in the vicinity or simply an indication that the fish were hungrier at that particular time. One spring in Rhode Island, at a point in the season when we were certain that the only stripers around were all schoolies, hits were so subtle that we could not feel them take. We only knew that *something* was chewing parts of our sea worms. Frankly, at the time I was convinced that we had been invaded by some sort of flea, incapable of telegraphing their presence. Yet, if you held your rod, there was barely discernible movement soon after a fresh bait hit the bottom. When we struck we fanned as though a fast ball had gone over the plate way ahead of the swing. It was kind of maddening. Finally, in frustration, I laid a fresh bait, a section of worm the size of a cigarette filter, on the bottom for 30 seconds and hauled back, waiting a like time before doing it again. This proved to pay off because I was hooking fish every cast after that.

Once you know what is doing it, and you are satisfied that you have at long last come upon a solution, it is easier to walk away from striped bass between 14 and 18 inches long. But the thing that has always evoked a measure of consternation in my mind is why they always must behave strangely in the same way at the same time, without regard for size.

How to feed the bait? When to strike? These questions suffer from less complexity. The key to the answer is that the baits we talk of here are castable. That is, because they are either worms or cut parts of forage species—mackerel, pogies, etc.—they are small enough that you *know* the fish has fully engulfed the entire bait if it is exerting tension upon the line; therefore, it is usually enough to have the line under tension with the reel in antireverse. Most often the hard takers in particular will set the hook upon themselves.

A good representation of top-notch striper lures await their trial by water.

≈ *Plugging the Beach* ≈

The great advantage in plugging the beach is that it covers water. You will find yourself confronted with two situations in which your search technique must be different: The first involves fishing long stretches of shore where you exercise what you know about looking for bass, cautiously metering your efforts to the best structure; and the second is taking up a position on some prominent spot where you have good reason to believe that the fish will pass and repeating your casts with the hope of intersecting them. This latter choice—if you apply what you learn in these pages—will probably be an inlet or prominent tiderip known to appeal to gamefish.

In such places current is not always in evidence, but it is more likely, so we will treat such moving water as an important element of the surfcasting situation. The relationship between such current and the positions of feeding gamefish is no small part of the angling picture.

All pelagics must face the current, or, if they are traveling, must swim at a faster speed than the water in order to provide a fresh passage of water through their gills. Naturally, in that situation they are less likely to see or be interested in your offer; more likely, these fish will cruise in a more leisurely way, facing the current and dropping back. When doing this they are usually on the lookout for bait as they rove. Places that appeal to them, either because of bottom structure or the attraction of bait, will often slow them down or cause them to take up a stationary position in the current.

Whatever the type of prominent location, there are often current edges, back eddies, boulders, or sandbars that are popular to the fish and continually hold them year in and year out. This is why experienced surfcasters will often have a favorite "stand" upon which they rely to provide them with a greater level of action. While it is unlikely that such hot spots would be devoid of other anglers, the more of these spots that you know, the more of them that you can work, hence increasing your yield.

Current also influences the artificial that you will be casting. All plugs are designed to work as a result of the passage of water upon them. In still waters the retrieve causes one kind of action with a given speed of retrieve, and such changes in speed, either slower or faster, dramatically alter the plug's performance; moreover, the variety of types of plugs at our disposal makes seriously different demands and requires entirely different responses to the influence of current. For instance, a subtle lure that has little action built into its design, and relies upon the fisherman to impart action, will suffer less influence from current. But those with swimmer plates, which are intended to cause a plug to slither from side to side, do so in direct proportion to the push of water upon it. When the speed of retrieve is added to that of the current, the plug too often swishes frantically from side to side. Such excessive action appeals to only the most aggressive of our quarry. It boils down to using much slower retrieves in fast water than one might along a casual, unpretentious stretch of beach. The fact is that fast-water spots are best fished by casting roughly 90 degrees from the shore and simply allowing the plug to drift under tension from the rod tip. At full tide, when current is at its peak, it may even be necessary to seek out quieter eddies where the plug will present itself as more alluring, less animated target.

Even wave action generates temporarily overly frantic currents where waters might otherwise be quite still. Keep in mind that a 4-footer, a level sea that we routinely fish, slides back downhill with enough force to put the plug into fits of commotion. As a result the wise caster imparts one retrieve speed on the outside and another, slower one, when his offer is drumming in the suds. There will be a point, sea depending, when stopping all retrieve is in your best interest. It is a case of feel and judgment. With some experienced anglers this feel is often a second nature, which they often find themselves at a loss to explain. This could be advanced as just one type of situation in which a person is catching fish and unable to share exactly what he or she is doing to enable companions to do the same. We hasten to add that the foam of the first wave is the last place a surfcaster should be fishing carelessly.

In any discussion on retrieve speed, no retrieve at all deserves a measure of attention. Many nights, when shining a light on the water to find a route along a treacherous bar's dropoff, or some other reason for such an unproductive indiscretion, I have noticed sand eels or sperling idling on the surface with their noses glued to the surface tension and their tails angled downward 20 degrees. We need not know why they are doing this, but it is important to recognize that the position is a natural one for them. Small swimming plugs that bear physical resemblance to these forage species will often work wonders by simply casting the lures and permitting them to lie idle in the same way; thus, we not only simulate size and appearance but behavior. If the plug is to be an effective imitation, it needs help from its caster.

The angler whose beach choice lacks the attractiveness of an inlet or promontory must hunt for the fish. If you have unlimited time and energy, then it would be a simpler matter to begin casting at point A and continue casting every few yards until you arrive at point B. But the realities are that such a game plan is unrealistically hard work, often without the slightest promise of success, so your first efforts should be geared to locating fish by sampling the surf at a spread of arbitrary points or by reading the structure of the beach for suitable bars, holes, or sloughs that will enable you to *determine the presence of gamefish* as efficiently as possible. Once you have done this competently (assuming that it can be done, because no technique can manufacture gamefish), you can make a judgment about whether to move on to another location. It is a hunting game.

Let us assume for a moment that you have found something. First, you must go on the premise that you are dealing with a school of fish. Very often, one fish is clear indication that there are others, so any contact—a bat on the plug, a rub, the feel of a turning fish, a strike, or the landing of a fish—is reason to intensify and tighten efforts at that location.

We have fished this way for many years, and once we located fish we always "farmed" the beach intensely. The term "farming" is one we coined ourselves for this type of fishing, which is put into play after the cursory mode. Farming is a term I use to describe casting, then stepping a few feet in one direction and casting again. The notion is born out of a vision one would have of dragging an offer every few inches in the way that a farmer would plow a field. The idea, of course, is that all water must be covered so as to present the plug over all possible yardage in the surf.

Once stripers are located a person could stand in one spot on a beach and produce contacts, but his efficiency is enhanced if he travels along seeking out what fish are lying in the surf spread arbitrarily along the shore. The caster, who is moving cautiously, will catch more. Always, when fish are located, a pattern emerges. You might find that when you move in a certain direction, say east, the level of activity is greater, or that most hits come close to the beach. Whatever thing distinguishes itself about the fishing that particular night at that particular place, the surfcaster who observes it is going to come out way ahead.

If you take into account all the different elements we've covered so far—speed of retrieve, plug choice, action, current, water depth, structure, and finally direction—the complexities of this fine sport emerge in an overwhelming diversity of variables that further illustrate how confounding surfcasting can be. Moreover, while you are agonizing over such choices, the tide, the wind, or the position of the moon are changing. And while it is frustrating at times, in its proper execution it can be beautiful.

POPPERS

I suffer from much ambivalence about popping plugs. It seems to me that few outstanding stripers, as a percentage of the great fish I have known, have been caught on them. At the same time we hasten to add that poppers are notoriously a daytime lure; consequently, the plugs themselves may not be the cause, but rather that time when they are in use.

On the other hand, there is the matter of surfcasting by day, and, all things considered, poppers seem to be the best plug to use if one is to cast under the influence of the sun. Despite my mixed feelings, I must confess that a popper gets the fish's attention. And if getting attention is more difficult in rough water with onshore winds, then there is no better way. There is much more to be said.

Surface poppers are our fastest-moving plugs. This indicates a need for a measure of skill to perfect an effective retrieve, particularly with conventional or revolving-spool equipment. Those who use high-speed reels of either type (conventional or spinning) and crank them too quickly are at risk of evoking interest in bass or blues, which are unable to catch the plug. Yet a loafing plug may not throw enough water at slow speeds, or, worse, sink and kill the entire retrieve. Hence, we walk a fine line where the plug should be hurrying, tossing water ahead of it, stirring up the surface, yet still be able to be caught by a pursuing gamefish. The challenge to accomplish this increases when fishing a heavy sea where the offer is climbing, then careening off the sides of breakers. When the water is taken into account, even a retrieve speed that is according to text can be altered outside

Poppers are created to imitate squid, which appear in abundance here on a striper beach.

the control of the surfcaster. The plug vacillates, therefore, through periods of being a suitable objective to being virtually impossible for any gamefish to overtake. This is why adjustments in retrieve speed are often necessary to keep a high percentage of the plug's return within the limits of catchability; nevertheless, in the height of this endeavor, the plug is often out of sight, forcing the fisherman to "feel" his way.

Gamefish will often stab viciously at the quarry, missing badly, or their effort—because it is a sea of accidents at this point—will appear as nothing more than a swirl behind the plug that could easily go unnoticed. For that reason, a watchful eye is needed to note any misses that occur. Such often subtle swirls can frequently be accommodated by dropping back or slowing to give the fish another shot. Such second shots, executed by a striper or blue that apparently feels like a failed warrior denied, are nearly always on target and more vicious.

Poppers are hard work, but the reward is a higher level of castability that is second only to that of metal lures. Indeed, if I suffer from any reservations about poppers being limited in their use for big stripers, it is more than compensated for by an overwhelming advantage in catching bluefish of all sizes.

That fact brings us to wire leaders, which, while not mandatory for leader protection from the teeth of bluefish, do offer a measure of insurance. In spite of all my qualifications about the use of wire, I have never been able to discern any reduced striper interest when wire was used ahead of poppers.

A great deal of attention is given, rightfully, to how well a surface plug pops, but there is another activity that most surfcasters overlook: its swim—the action of side-to-side movement imparted between pops.

I was first acquainted with this function during an accidental meeting with Bob Pond, inventor and manufacturer of Atom plugs, on Massachusetts's Horseneck Beach more than twenty years ago. He was testing a new design of swimmer, and I was working a popper that had been made by someone else. His first question upon examining it was, "Does it swim?" And I, thinking that he had misidentified the thing, reminded him that it was a popper. Pond patiently went on to explain that if it was a suitable popper it would "swim" between pops. Sure enough, he demonstrated by moving my plug through the surf at about the speed that you would move a swimmer. It then moved side to side while under the tension of retrieve.

Not too long after that, one early-autumn afternoon I was casting a moderate surf at Point Judith into a sea that was *known* to have school stripers. I had caught two or three, but there was a pair of fellows standing side by side on a nearby stone who were each catching three bass to my one. The better they did, and they were obviously casting poppers, the more frantic I made my retrieve. It embarrasses me to remember how long it took me to realize that they were barely cranking their reels. Really, what stands out in my memory the most was how they kept stringing those bass on a length of clothesline that had become so heavy that each breaker would tug dangerously upon one of them. By the time I knew what I should do, the fish moved on. When we met on the shore, I noticed that they were both using Striper Swipers, which are made by Pond, and judging from the retrieve that I had seen them use, they had been *swimming* the plugs.

SWIMMERS

The swimming plug, usually equipped with a plate forward to execute the side-to-side swimming action, is preeminently a nighttime offer. Because this is when we do most of our fishing, swimmers are the most important family of artificials in the surfcaster's bag.

A typical swimmer has variable swimming action, often within the same model, is subsurface, riding only a few inches deep, floats when at rest, and is equipped with two or three sets of treble hooks. When compared to poppers or metal, they tend to cast rather badly, but there is a strong reverse correlation between castability and their effectiveness, which we will enumerate more closely later.

Swimmers are the lure of choice for most night stripermen.

Earlier in this section it was necessary to delve into the influence of passing water upon the action of a swimmer. We said that this occurred because of two influences: the speed of retrieve and the speed of current. A decision had to be made as to where this dynamics of swim treatment should be placed, because it was necessary in the understanding of where as well as how swimmers should be fished. Reiteration is no sin when talking of things this important.

It is neither desirable nor necessary to go into a plug-by-plug dissertation, because of the many manufacturers and models involved. One need only have an understanding of a few basic types and their particular idiosyncrasies.

For instance, Dannys, Atoms, Goo-goo eyes, and many more are all rather large; they are equipped with metal swimming plates, weigh about the same, and produce similar effects and results. Then there are unique swimmers, like the Giant Pikie Minnow, which have to be treated separately. Finally, Finland plugs deserve a section of their own.

I was going to say more about swimming action. Among the larger swimmers, the 3-ounce Atom, which is 9 inches long with a metal swimmer plate, is often preferred for conventional or heavy spinning. There are any number of similar plugs molded in plastic or fashioned of wood, which emit similar swimming action. In most instances the rule is to swim or retrieve these slowly, thus avoiding an overly frenzied action. Some surfcasters believe they can adjust the swimming action by varying the angle of the swim plate, but if the adjustments are made badly a plug's action can be ruined entirely. Moreover, tonight's perfect action may be a curse tomorrow when the waves or currents are different.

When we speak of swimming action, no action at all is an alternative that deserves some consideration. I can think of any number of times when plugs were allowed to sit on a placid surf until a bass, apparently watching from below, perhaps fuming over some perceived territorial transgression, rose slowly to blow it up.

Years ago after a blitzy night with a buggy full of New York surfmen fishing with us on the Cape, one went down to the water after it was all over, threw a blue Atom, which landed on the surface with a mighty splash, and let it lay.

After nearly a minute of quiet flotation, he popped the thing violently, then let it lay in silence again. When he repeated the maneuver a second time, a 40-pound lineside came up and took it down as though it were a marine Twinkie. I would have dismissed the incident as a fluke were it not for the other two of comparable size that he subsequently landed. Moreover, it was something that he had done before. It is a downside-up world when we swim poppers and "pop" swimmers.

Plugs don't catch stripers, surfcasters do. Earlier I mentioned how the surf in the last wave can increase the motion of swim in a plug. Sometimes when the surf is light, or when a plug happens to be coming ashore between combers, speeding up the retrieve will evoke a strike. I have often thought that such *changed* motion was sending a message to a stalking striper that the bait fish knew it was under attack and was trying to execute an escape. This raises questions as to whether it is the threat of an escaping bait fish, or is it the first wave, harboring a greater number of fish, that makes these last yards as productive as they are.

That is not to say that all surf fishing takes place under the influence of the first wave. Indeed, anyone who spends his night scratching the shore with short lobs is overreacting to a truth, which, while basic, has limitations. In surfcasting, a game of limitations, including many that are self-imposed, you should exercise all your options. Many currents or spicy bits of structure, as well as passing gamefish, are a good distance from the beach. So ends one spatial dimension.

Sinking Swimmers

Swimmers that drift to the bottom when at rest do so usually with the help of lead that is built in or added by anglers who choose to alter them. While such plugs are less important in the overall application of swimmers, there are places where they do outperform their more buoyant counterparts. Of course such "loaded" plugs cast a little better and can be relied upon to swim in a more subdued fashion, but their greatest advantage is that if they are cast slightly upstream and the retrieve is delayed as well as slowed, they will run at greater depth for a brief period at the beginning of the retrieve. In strong tiderips over deep water, knowing surfcasters will often pump them gently without retrieving an inch of line, permitting them to dance about in the currents until they are nearly against the downstream beach before a hasty retrieve is initiated.

The loading of plugs is accomplished in other ways. New York and New Jersey surfcasters are fond of using mercury, because in its liquid form it moves about within the plug, changing the point of balance, quietly. Conversely, lead shot is popular with some, because it can be installed through a small hole while being counted upon to rattle within hollow, plastic bodies, emitting sound. Plastic-cast swimmers are usually hollow with chambers that are separated by plastic walls.

The old-time Reverse Atom came through with holes in the rear chamber, which filled with water, enhancing castability while subduing action. The "Reverse," as it is fondly called, started out as an Atom swimmer that some enterprising or very drunk surfcaster attached at the tail hook mount and installed a treble at the plug's eye. This turning around of the plug had the effect of causing the plug to slither on the top from side to side in a very enticing surface commotion that rendered the thing more like a popper. The Reverse never had the fame of more widely known poppers, but at times it has brought bass up when nothing else would and it causes bluefish to pant. Remember that if you are ever caught at daybreak on a blitzy beach with a bagful of swimming plugs.

The rise in use of loaded plugs might have come from a leak in a plastic plug. (Such speculations are mindful of how man started eating cooked meat.) Indeed, manufacturing flaws, which permit water infusion, are common. Such leakers, when they are not intended and, worse, when they go undetected, can destroy the effectiveness of a lure with an otherwise impeccable reputation. Many a surfcaster has spent a night beside friends who were hammering fine fish, while nothing would improve his plight, only to discover at dawn that the poor surfcaster's swimmer had been scratching the bottom. And, I suppose, in all fairness, many a "killer" has been at a loss to explain his or her success at the time, only to find that the "miracle plug" was an ounce heavier than it was supposed to be. It is a door that swings both ways. Failures or successes that are unexplained or unplanned are a sign that the fisherman involved has no control over the situation. The difference between a lucky fisherman and a good one is that the latter knows what he is doing. Still, Lady Luck is an old friend.

I once had a dandy loaded plug: a loaded Junior Atom, a type Bob Pond only made a few of. Three ounces it weighed and sank like a rock. The ordinary model floated at rest, swam well, and enjoyed a noble reputation as a catcher of striped bass. Meanwhile, the loaded job, weighing in at 3 ounces, did none of those things. The first time that I used it was on a Columbus weekend at Green Hill, Rhode Island, during an icy dawn that had little promise. I can't even tell you why I was using it, because the water there isn't deep enough to require a deep run. Worse, I didn't know a whole lot about surf fishing, though I thought I did at the time. Anyway, during the dull glow in the east something took it and ran out some line that was restored until the thing was flailing right in the wash. Once I tried pressuring it there, but my timing was bad, and the downward force of a receding wave, when combined with what the bass was doing, could have broken it off. Next foamer I pressed it again just as it curled and broke, and a huge fish slid high to my feet. Reaching down to grasp the gill cover, I heard a tinkle in the gravel from the sound of my swimming falling loose. I never did know where I had hooked that 52-pounder.

I reacted to the success about like anybody else would, but I never really credited the plug. Unaccountably the creation lay in a tackle valise of my buggy for three years before I used it again. To me the great fish it had taken was more a stroke of luck.

Three miles west, on East Beach, Charlestown, I came out one sunset in 1969 to plug. I had been fishing eels all season with considerable success, but that particular night I just felt like plugging. I recall it occurring to me while readying tackle that this was the plug that had taken my last 50-pounder three seasons before. I remember reasoning that there was no point in saving the thing simply for sentimental reasons while I installed new trebles. Mostly, though, I remember everyone's astonishment and my own agonized effort at trying to dismiss the event as routine, when a *second* 52-pounder lay on the beach in front of the gang there.

You would think, what with two great fish in as many nights, that I would climb the highest dune and sing praises for loaded swimmers. Still, like the other things we fish with, each has its place.

COLOR

Surfcasters are both a sentimental and superstitious lot. Many will catch a fish on a light blue plug, then swear that striped bass will take nothing else. Then they will be beside some fellow mohawking linesides with a different model plug, but which is pink, and they are converted to worshiping pink. I've even known a fellow on the Cape who swore by fluorescent orange for use on deep, dark nights. Such aberrations dwell more in the mind than in the annals of science. What then can we say about colors? Nothing that is concrete.

The reason is that to some degree the prophecies fulfill themselves. When amber is hot the word gets out about amber, and everybody is fishing amber. With everybody fishing amber, all fish caught are caught on amber. Then somebody tires of amber, catches a large number of fish because he did something else right, and amber is dead. With the choice of color so solidly influenced more by social considerations, I have never been able to determine any solid relationship between success and the color preferences of striped bass, though, admittedly, I have vacillated through love affairs over color myself.

I am hopelessly partial to realistic paint jobs. To me if a

thing is intended to look like a bait fish, after its shape and action, the least we can do is darken the back while leaving a white belly. In a sense, plugs are to surfcasters what flies are to trout fishermen, and the latter wouldn't dream of drifting a tan insect when trout bellies are stuffed with black ones. Fly fishermen call it the school of realism.

Years ago during a period when monster stripers were feeding off the Cape's Nauset Beach, we found the fish were gorging themselves on foot-long mackerel. Back then, the late sixties, few plugs had a mackerel paint job; the only one that I knew was the Gibbs Trolling Swimmer, a lathe-turned wood creation that had been developed for trolling but cast moderately well. We murdered bass with the thing while standing in a dry crowd fishing known proven killers. The fishless stood both astonished at its success and horrified at the use of a boatman's plug by a surfcaster. Of course it could have been the plug's action, rather than the mackerel paint job. Again we were unable or unwilling to isolate variables.

As a result of that success, I began painting the dark vermiculations that so characterize the mackerel's coloration on many of my swimming plugs. It seemed to me that they caught more bass than those models that remained unadorned by this touch of realism. As a result I developed an article that appeared in the July 1970 issue of *Salt Water Sportsman*, called "Flavor It Mackerel." Around the same time I sent off a letter to Plastics Research, makers of the Rebel plug, urging them—because their plugs already utilized realism in their painting—to offer a mackerel rendition. In response the chairman of the board said that the idea was under serious consideration. I'll never know how influential my ideas were, but Rebels with mackerel paint jobs soon followed. So much for color.

MORE TACTICS

Most of the time standard killers will take striped bass from the beach if they are there. Often these fish will exhibit a pickiness, a selectivity in feeding, that can leave many of us retching in the foreshore. When it is like this, linesides bulging the sea behind our plugs, fish all over the place but few being taken, it is commonly a sound option to resort to small, sensitive little offers that either raise less bioluminescence or better simulate the bait at hand. We'll talk more about that later. But what if the standard alternative, which is meant to deal with this selectivity, fails to win them over?

Having seen the gang hurriedly switch to lighter rods and lines to cast lighter, smaller plugs in order to fish closer to the beach, I can attest to the occasional group frustration that besets itself when the "cure" fails.

Sometimes, only sometimes, the biggest plug in your bag will move linesides when nothing else can. And the largest striper plug that I know of is the Creek Chub Giant Pikie Minnow, a two-piece jointed creation that is 13 inches long and weighs 4 ounces. Known fondly among surfcasters as the "jointed eel," the thing was developed for freshwater use on big pike and muskie and was never intended to simulate an eel at all; moreover, it bears only a slight resemblance, its proportions too short and heavy for that mission. It is, however, a frantic swimmer, combining its swim plate–generated action with the two-bodied jointed characteristic, which causes it to virtually slither through the water. But we hasten to emphasize that this monster must be fished slowly, and the angler must be constantly aware of the water in which it is being used.

The jointed eel is both tiring and painful to cast because of its weight and wind resistance. Strained muscles truly are not unusual with those who use it regularly. It is commonly thought to be too large for many of the stripers and blues that are about; however, I have frequently seen 4-pounders of both species—scarcely twice the length of the plug—hammer the Pikie. Such outlandish response to this chunk of wood gives rise to a couple of theories about plugs that may contribute in some way to your overall view of plug fishing.

I have occasionally heard that bass will strike a plug, not because it is a single fish, but rather because it is a pod of them swimming in close formation. Certainly the fact that a schoolie would strike the oversize jointed eel without hesitation lends some credence to the idea. The other suspicion I have mulled over the years is that of propensity within gamefish. I'll elaborate. Within a given group of fish, there will always be a number to which a particular action or type of lure is more attractive, more irresistible. As such fish age, expanding their exposure to the efforts of man to catch them, those with such a propensity are taken; thus, as a particular lure technique becomes more widely used, the proportion of available fish with a propensity for that lure technique narrows. As a consequence anglers who use what everybody else is using are either fishing for a small group of survivors or relegated to the younger, less experienced, of a species. I have often thought this about popping plugs, because of their widespread use and the relatively small number of large striped bass to their credit. Conversely, many of the new lures, say like needlefish, don't necessarily slay stripers because of some special characteristic in their makeup; they are what they are because the striper population largely has never seen them before, and the fish with a propensity for taking them are an untapped population.

To tie all this together, the Giant Pikie might be such a good plug simply because it is not widely used, and it never will be because it is too large for most surfcasters to fish. When a bass sees one go by, it is something that he has never seen before. Of course both concepts—plugs that are perceived as a pod of bait and that of propensity—may be admittedly highly speculative trappings of a plug fisherman's mind. Let's get back to more concrete observations.

The behavior of every living thing upon this planet is tied directly to a host of natural adaptations that have evolved from its environment. This is why one can observe such differences between species. Naturally, our interest here is in making comparisons, as well as isolating differences, in how the striped bass and bluefish behave. It is particularly important in this section to examine closely the diverse feeding habits of the two.

My wife, Joyce, landed this lineside after it took a Rebel.

Striped bass engulf their prey, swallowing it whole. If it is large they must take it down head first so as to fold fins and dorsals back against the bait fish's body. Were they to fail to do so, the bait could become hopelessly lodged in the throat of the attacking fish. I have known this to happen with large bass feeding upon hickory shad that weighed up to 4 pounds. No doubt the need for a head-first orientation of the bait may sometimes be accommodated by turning the thing within the mouth. More likely the predator has honed its skills to the point where it can seize prey and turn it in one motion; consequently, stripers are headhunters. When we apply this fact to the plugs that we are using, you will notice that many of the bass caught on plugs are taken with the front hook. The small percentage taken on either the belly or tail hook may in fact be mere accidents where the front treble was dislodged. As an aside, many surfmen I've known expressed surprise at plugs draped upon the head or gill covers of fish without realizing that the plug had been expelled during the fight, but the treble remained within the mouth; therefore, the front hook of any plug is going to have more use with stripers.

Because a plug is a solid member, lacking the flexibility of a meaty bait, there are occasional, accidental fulcrums created by the arbitrary placement of the plug and treble hook within the jaw. Such accidents of physics at times position a plug in such a way that the forces involved can pry the steel, straightening hooks easily, particularly the front ones. Indeed, such forces can be so great that the 5/0 treble of a pikie, a size that is difficult to buy, can be forced wide open. I once resorted to 6/0 hooks on the front of that plug and still had bass straighten them. Of course the rate of incidence declines as the hook is enlarged. Unaccountably, some plugs suffer from this more than others. Surprisingly, I have yet to see one manufacturer offer a product with a larger front hook. On average I find it necessary to enlarge front hooks by one size.

This measure also serves to subdue overly zealous swimming plugs, which is a greater curse than dull movement. The big hook also adds to casting weight, which is welcome with swimming plugs.

When bluefish feeding technique is examined, we see an entirely different adaptation. This species relies upon the activity of a school for feeding. Here the digestive process starts sooner, with the teeth. Blues will drive bait into one another, maiming as they go. They tend to target the tail, immobilizing their quarry, which drift helplessly after attack to be picked up either by other blues or fish that turn for a second pass. In sharp contrast to stripers, blues are taking a plug from the other end, which elevates the tail hook as the prominent one to be served by the attentions of the fisherman. I think that placement of the rear hook offers a lower incidence of accidental levers that would straighten steel. Blues have more muscular jaws, however. Thus, beefing up the tail hook on any plug—swimmer or popper—is justified. Of course we say these things under the assumption that the angler is going to know what will strike next.

FINNISH SWIMMERS

We have purposely separated the Finnish swimmers from the other swimmers for two reasons: First, their advent, when compared to the others, is relatively new, and, because of this, there is a great deal more to be said; moreover, this special family of plugs revolutionized the quality and effectiveness of plug fishing, bringing it to what we have come to know today.

More than fifty years ago Lauri Rapala of Vaaksy, Finland, began hand carving his swimming plugs of balsa wood in large enough quantities to sell to friends. Rapala had a reputation both for catching fish and building outstanding lures, and those available for market were bought up quickly for their freshwater application. It was not until the late 1950s that Rapala's creations found their way onto this continent through the visionary efforts of Ron Weber, founder of Normark Corporation in Minnesota. It took five years for surfcasters to discover the things. About that time *Life* magazine carried an interesting piece portraying Rapala's unique skills as a carver of plugs. Not too long after that, I paid some serious folding green—twice what was charged for any other plug—for one of his swimmers.

At the time we had been in the habit of casting for school stripers behind Long Bar on Cape Cod's Nauset Beach. Each night when the rising tide drove us off the bar, the small bass would show, and we would take them with a variety of Atoms and Darters; however, the night when I first cast the Rapala, a slim, freshwater version of balsa no more than 5 inches long, the results were way beyond anything that I had ever experienced while plugging the striper surf. It could have been simply an accident of the night were it not for the fact that my catch was better than any of the others', and they knew as much if not more than I of the movements of bass in this particular situation. There was no question in my mind that I had come upon a "secret weapon." That is not to say that I discovered the Rapala in the striper's territory, only that I had brought it to the small, esoteric group of stripermen with which I was acquainted. I was soon to learn that other groups of surfcasters throughout the Striper Coast were finding out the same things about Rapala's plugs.

Along with being expensive the Rapala cast badly, because it suffered from both poor aerodynamics and light weight. The early models often broke in half while being thrashed about by a wild striper. Hook mountings tore free, and swimmer plates would be crunched off. We both cursed and loved them at the same time, because there was nothing that you could throw that did a better job of tempting linesides. Until then striper plugs were either made of wood or badly cast in plastic. All were round and fat, doing virtually nothing to imitate the various bait fish that stripers fed upon, notably the sand eel.

Sand eels are found along sandy beaches throughout the striper's range on north to Labrador. Many locations, particularly Cape Cod, will host this bait species in such great numbers that they often can be found disturbing many acres of the sea's surface. They are a slender fish with a body that is roughly one-tenth as high as it is long. We have already covered them extensively in the bait section of this book (pages 127–63) so we only emphasize here those characteristics relating to their importance as both striper forage and their accidental imitation by the plug from Finland.

The Rapala stood out because for the first time we were casting an artificial that simulated this important bait fish. Length-versus-thickness proportions were off slightly, at probably eight to one, but still came closer than anything heretofore known; moreover, the Rapala enjoyed greater realism with its dark back, a suggestion of silver along the flanks, and white belly. This plug was truly a sand eel–simulating offer.

Within two years of the Rapala's debut on the Striper Coast, Plastics Research of Arkansas marketed the Rebel. Their model of plug was a production casting of plastic, however, that bore all the dimensional qualities needed for effective sand-eel simulation without the prohibitive costs of hand-carved creations. Moreover, the plastic bodies proved to be more resilient to the rigors of sea fishing than balsa. Again it would delight me to be able to say that we discovered the Rebel's application to striper fishing, but others recognized the Rebel's value independently, as is so often the case.

This brings to mind a similar situation that might have been happening in plug manufacturing. Was Plastics Research seeking to imitate the Rapala? Or did the Rebel come as an inevitable development from the similar thought patterns of fishermen? True, the need for a slim swimming plug should have been evident to any competent observer. On the other hand the Rebel followed on the heels of the Rapala. The differences in production processes and material should be enough to render the Rebel a solely separate fishing lure. I am not sure if it is even important to speculate about this, and I doubt, what with litigation a possibility, that there would be any point in seeking a truthful answer from a more well placed source. Our purpose here, after all, is to chronicle the development of our most effective striper plug.

Before too many years a host of manufacturers were offering a slim, molded-plastic swimmer that provided startlingly similar effects and results, sharing in a plug market that went far beyond striper fishing. To name some in a rapidly expanding market, at the risk of overlooking a few: Bombers, Nils Masters, and Red Fins.

Another inevitable development within this group of plugs was the evolutionary variations that came from advanced development. Sizes now run from 2 to 8 inches in length and up to more than 2 ounces in weight. They are available in both floating and loaded models, straight and jointed, with a variety of colors offered for just about every important species this side of tuna.

Fishing with Finnish Swimmers

Because of the many different types of "Finnish" plugs, fishing them properly is fraught with complexities that we must deal with at length here. Every consideration that distinguishes one model of plug from another involves trade-offs. For instance, a loaded sinking plug will comb deep, fast-running tiderips more effectively, and it will cast farther, but it does not have the swimming action of its floating counterpart. The latter consideration has done nearly as much to make this type of plug distinctive as has the slim length. Indeed, I have found few places where a loaded Rebel or Rapala was worth that serious a trade-off. On the other hand, I have also found big bass in the shallows rooting for sand eels that could not even see a passing subsurface swimmer because of the way they were feeding. When that was the case, a long slim plug that scratched the bottom often brought vicious strikes. Still, overall the unloaded, floating plugs are best.

Our efforts should be toward imitation of the forage species. For that reason small plugs have an edge. Two basic sizes dominate the striper-fishing market: 5½ inches and 7 inches. The 7-inch model is often much larger than the sand eels upon which bass are feeding, and, because of its size, the error in proportion—eight to one—is exaggerated. It has always been easier to fool even large stripers with the small plug, but never forget that the danger of hook failure increases with smaller trebles, and an onshore wind or red-hot tiderip on the outside may force a choice to the larger model. Also, what if the bait at hand are mackerel or pogies? Then the surfcaster should choose the larger plug.

Jointed members of the family are known to produce astonishing results. Because what we really have here are two plugs connected, the action is multiplied. Fast-water rips or heavy seas can promote excessive or overly frantic action. Flat-water nights, however, when the fish are picky, a slow enticing retrieve, stopping often to lie still, can produce more fish than other methods.

Fishing with these plugs carries a unique set of problems with which one does not have to deal otherwise. Hooks are straightened, swimmer plates are broken off by strikes, and some makes are even manufactured so that they leak and take on water to become sinkers. So often there has been a gang of us on the beach, all taking fish with the same plug, and one guy is crying because he can't buy a hit using the same thing everybody else is. If it happens to you, inspect your plug to be sure that it is all there and doing what it was meant to.

Among the many curses of Finnish plugs not to be overlooked are the horrible casting qualities. Ideal saltwater plugs should weigh more than 2 ounces, which precludes the use of many models that we so highly recommend. Worse, surfcasters whose preference is conventional or revolving-spool tackle are nearly all excluded from fishing the things at all, because they require close to 3 ounces, a weight that is not even offered on the market. True, if you're a highly skilled conventional angler, you can fish the larger, 2-ounce ones, but it is an individual's choice in an already complicated field of decisions.

Spinning tackle is far and away the best choice for use with this special group of plugs. Using the 5½-inch floater, which weighs ½ ounce, the range of suitable line sizes ends at 20-pound test. No terminal tackle should be anywhere above the plug; the line should be tied direct to the plug's eye. Never use a wire leader on any Finland-type plug if you hope to catch stripers! There are of course situations, if the bass in evidence are running on the small side, when "schoolie tackle" is more comfortable fishing. Naturally, lighter lines of say 10- or 12-pound cast the ½ ounce more comfortably. At the same time never forget this thing about saltwater fishing: Great striped bass roam our seas without regard for the dominant sizes of their brethren. I do not care to count the times when all the surfmen on the beach were hauling away on small fish when the report of parting monofilament broke the hiss of falling waves like a rifle shot. And even those who knew how to handle great fish with gossamer lines could not prevent a turn of line from being wrapped around the flexing body, its sharp scales bristling, of a moby striped bass.

When Lauri Rapala was posthumously enshrined as the 1985 electee to the National Fresh Water Fishing Hall of Fame, I wonder if anyone was thinking of his contribution to surfcasting or to the ever-widening "family" of swimming plugs for which I am sure he is responsible.

TEASERS OR DROPPERS

By definition a teaser or dropper is a small lure that trails off the line above the larger lure, which acts as a casting weight. Two theories are in widespread belief regarding such droppers: 1) Gamefish have a choice between the two sizes; 2) The larger lure, which is trailing the smaller one, lends authenticity to the presentation, because the larger appears to be stalking the smaller one. Both are interesting theories, but I subscribe to neither, because I have seen too many instances when the larger offer's only function was to act as a casting weight. Indeed, it is difficult to think any other way when all, or most, of the fish coming in have latched onto the teaser. Still, we must assess any comparisons between the effectiveness of the two more in terms of which types of teaser and plug. Certainly, bad plugs or ineffective teasers lend too much variability to any assessments of the combination system we speak of here.

The teasers of thirty years ago were crude, unsophisticated offerings. I vividly recall two that I wish I could forget. Surf-casters of the time used to lash a strip of pork rind to a 6/0 hook. If you happened to forget the pork rind after fishing, or used other tackle and let the thing hang in the bumper spike of your buggy too long, the pork would dry out and harden like plastic. The other was a pinch of white bucktail lashed down to the throat of the hook. The failing of the bucktail flies was that they rarely had the adequate length to provide the proportions exhibited by sand eels. I believe that is why the pork rind had a slight edge over bucktail in assessing droppers of the time, because the pork, for all its failings, at least was longer and thinner.

Roughly twenty years ago I introduced the eel fly dropper. This was between four and seven white saddle hackle feathers lashed to a 3/0 stainless hook. We sometimes resorted to using black feathers, which did catch a worthy number of stripers, but I never felt that black was a suitable application of realism, what with so many sand eels about sporting white bellies. Later, we added green, gray, and black feathers in order to achieve the color gradient that is found in real animals, but I found no measurable difference in performance. Consequently, changing feathers while at the tying bench was not a worthwhile interruption. It was necessary to utilize stainless steel in the hook choice—though I disliked both the danger to lost fish and the added expense—because carbon steel hooks, with their inherent rust quality, tended to stain the feathers after one use. More should be said about my claim in introducing the eel fly.

There is nothing startlingly original or unique about changing dropper materials from bucktail to chicken feathers. Indeed, it was the obvious and sequentially natural step that might come to anyone who sought to enhance progression of the technique. The truth is that no such fly existed among the

This bass took the casting weight, but I've seen many nights when all fish the teaser.

tackle offers of the time. In my article published in *Salt Water Sportsman* in 1974, I was the first to espouse the virtue of feathers in droppers. Still, while I cling to the claim, I suspect the development was taking place independently elsewhere, possibly at a hundred places at once.

Red Gills

My intense interest in teasers was further heightened in 1975 when an English surf fisherman and distance caster visiting here left me some small lures that were developed and manufactured in his country. Called "Red Gills," they were 6 inches long, molded-rubber replicas of the sand eel with a narrow hollow portion, which permitted proper placement of the hook and passage of the leader through the head. The most unique aspect of the design was that the lure was equipped with a swimmer plate in the tail, which caused it to swim violently, imparting life within it—a quality heretofore unknown in our teasers. While the product's purpose had been to act as a teaser for jigging in deep water from boats—"wreck fishing"—it was evident that the thing had potential as a casting teaser from the beach. We subsequently learned that the red gill indeed was a worthy dropper for the striper surf.

My English friend had left only a handful, but that winter I wrote to Alex Ingram, the British manufacturer, and arranged to acquire a hefty supply. In his "care package" he included a number of the larger model, which I had not known of, that were 7½ inches long. He also said that he had a smaller model under development, which we later learned was roughly 4 inches.

Whatever can be said of the earlier covered eel fly, I claim first knowledge and use of the Red Gill in North America with more pride and far less reservation. It has since stormed fishing here for the very application that I first recognized: as a teaser or dropper for surfcasting stripers. (The idea had crossed my mind to seek the import rights at the time.)

Aside from the failure of the stainless hook with which it

was equipped, and which we quickly learned to replace, the Red Gill brought a new problem to the fore: relative weight in a teaser. Up to that point what teasers that we had used had been weightless. But the newfound British version had just enough weight and wind resistance to create some difficulty in casting, which reduced our choices in choosing a plug for the overall mission of delivery. We then learned, because it had never before been a problem, that larger plugs went a greater distance in alleviating the influence of a teaser upon casting distances. Still, we viewed this somewhat as a compromise, because our perception of dropper fishing was that the plug was still a worthy contributor to fish in the box. In reality it was a small price to pay.

Onshore winds are the caster's curse, in spite of their contribution of better fishing. Still, each fishing situation is different. While there may be many instances in which rolling linesides will be in the first wave, thus negating all need to consider distance, there are often times when casting distance is required to reach a tiderip or choice yardage of beach structure. Teasers, their bulk, size, and weight depending, do nothing to enhance the mission of reaching suitable yardages from the shore, despite their effectiveness in fishing. Thus, the surfcaster faces the age-old paradox of trade-offs.

Earlier when we praised the virtues of Finland-type swimmers, we ranked them as the best striper plugs. We thus begin by placing the most effective plugs in the casting-weight function of delivering teasers. Admittedly, half-ounce to just over 1-ounce plugs will rarely cast more than 60 feet, but that may be all you needed. Then, as distance requirements increase, you can up the weights and aerodynamics of plugs to meet the distance challenge. A continuum of options thus falls into place, as surfcasters end up casting Polaris poppers, Rabbits, or Gibbs Swimmers into an onshore gale merely for the delivery of the teaser.

My most notable experiences of that kind took place on the Cape's Race Point during such howling tempests. There I have seen 50-knot onshore winds turn the water white for as far as you could see. The only salvation for the spot was that currents that originated in deep water swept the silted surf clean with new water. In every instance where we faced this situation, virtually no casters fished, though there were many who wanted to. Snapping on 5-ounce bank sinkers in place of plugs, and using eel flies for their superior wind-resistant qualities, we frequently hammered stripers of all sizes. How could they see such a small fly in such a maelstrom? Don't question things that work.

Surfcasting offers a myriad of mix-and-match combinations that both suit the demands of stripers and the ever-changing perceptions of their pursuers. In earlier text we praised the live eel as a superior live bait to be "plugged." Anyone who is unable to grapple with the decision of whether to use live eels or teasers would do well to use a live eel as the delivery weight; however, because one has no way of knowing what bait is being taken, it is best to simply haul back on the take to cover both possibilities.

Too many surfcasters I have known sought to simplify dropper rigs by keeping them as short as possible. The logic is there, because the very idea of having *two* lures in the fore is fraught with difficulties. Poor aerodynamics aside, it is common to find the plug and teaser married, hook to hook, upon completion of a retrieve; all of us have been known to snag a rod guide on the cast, causing the whole thing to splat harmlessly in the surf at our fore. The situation underlines the basic fact that the more equipment in use, the more difficulties can and will arise. True, the shorter a rig is the less these difficulties will present themselves, but short leaders offer a far less desirable set of circumstances that impede the effectiveness of your setup.

You will find that with short, close-in setups frequent maulings occur: You feel something crawl all over your lures, haul back, then miss. What happens is that the bass will bump the plug while striking the teaser. Or when he takes the dropper his jaws will close either upon the terminal swivel or the trailing line to the plug. It is also easy to imagine, though difficult to prove, that contact with the plug while on the fish's body, when it is taking the teaser, has the effect of spooking the fish to the point where it aborts the take. Such bad takes are all indications of interference on the part of the other lure upon the strike that was targeted toward the dropper.

For these reasons the distance from the terminal to the plug *must* be at least 5 feet. The line falling from the terminal—that which attaches to the dropper—should be about 15 inches. This solves two problems: The taker can mouth the teaser without making contact with the plug in most cases, and there is enough line between the teaser and its terminal for the mouth to close upon it freely. I say "most cases" in the 5-foot section, because under tension your rig will have 45 inches of space between the dropper and plug/weight. This distance is only enough for a 20-pound fish to slip into with 5 inches to spare it from touching the plug with its body on the strike. You can easily see that the problems of dealing with larger bass, say 50 inches or so, demand even greater distances between the lures and their terminal. Keep in mind that each inch added to the dropper would necessitate another inch added to the plug's leader. True, these distances may sound unwieldy, because it is the custom, much to my chagrin, for surfcasters to swing their rods mightily with but 2 feet of line trailing from their tips, failing to put to work for them the laws of physics and centrifugal force, which would so enhance their casting skills. Thus, if people were fishing right in the first place, 5-foot leaders would be no handicap at all.

I can sing two more praises of the teaser or dropper: The single hook of the teaser has superior hooking qualities that are unfettered by the fulcrumlike nature of trebles on plugs mentioned earlier (pages 165–69), and, lest we overlook the most obvious, a higher percentage of bass will usually fall to the teaser. Still, the smaller group that takes the plug presents a danger that could be easily forgotten: that of dealing with a feisty gamefish bouncing on the beach as you reach down to subdue it. It is easy to recognize that the teaser, which is not engaged, could penetrate any part of your face. While this has never happened to me, in spite of hundreds of such encounters, I have often felt the feathers or rubber tickle my cheek or forehead, causing me to reel back in understandable concern.

We must next devote some space to the leader material used in such rigs. If you are certain you will be casting into a sea of bluefish, then you can set up a dropper rig of wire. I would avoid doing so, however, if there is the slightest chance that there may be stripers around. It is to your advantage to use slightly larger mono for the rigs than that used for your casting line. There is a great deal of stress and abrasion upon dropper rigs that would dictate that. Still, the lighter any lines are—casting or rigging—the less likely one is to tip off a selectively feeding gamefish. Most choices with which I would agree would be 30-pound leader material on rigs fished with 20-pound line and 40-pound leaders for those fishing 30-pound lines. However, and here come the trade-offs, what if *two* bass latch onto dropper and plug?

Roughly twenty years ago, when we family-fished with four kids, we came upon a large number of bass in the surf at Race Point. My wife, Joyce, our four kids, and I were casting into a moderate onshore wind with plugs and teasers when one of them brought in a fish somewhere in the 20s. Never letting the kids handle the fish out of fear that one of them might get hurt, I was removing it when I noticed that she had no plug. This raised no suspicion as I bent another on, except that I had a back-of-the-mind feeling that one of the others had suffered the mysterious disappearance of her teaser, perhaps some other night. Things were hot and heavy, and I forgot about the whole thing and went back down to the water before another of them caught a fish. Stripers were everywhere.

Hooking up immediately, my fish thrashed on the surface as I pressed it with a heavy conventional outfit that had 45-pound braided line. Except for a little extra water thrown on the surface, it seemed to be an average fish, 20s to 30s. To my astonishment there were two linesides in the surf! This of course solved the riddle of disappearing plugs and droppers.

What the kids apparently had done was hook two fish at once, one on each offer; however, their lighter, 30-pound leaders thought to be heavy enough for 20-pound spinning outfits were unable to take the dead-end strain of a pair of linesides going in opposite directions. Mine, tied together with 50-pound mono, was capable of absorbing such forces. We never kept accurate records of such doubles, but, as I recall, Joyce did have 41- and 36-pound fish doubled up during another tide another year. We subsequently all took doubles of fish over 20 pounds and under 40.

While the modern teasers that we have addressed at this point are limited to the red-gill and eel fly, I am certain that technological development, as well as a broader appreciation for their application, have put the technique on the threshold of explosion. Advanced and more widespread application of molding techniques, as well as more sophisticated, more supple materials, which did not even exist fifteen years ago, have found a niche in their application as fishing lures. Curly tails, Mr. Twisters, rubber worms, to name only a few that come to mind, are light enough, effective enough, and certainly cheap enough to find their way into the teaser application. If you are innovative and have a penchant for experimentation, you can thus concoct any number of teaser applications that will match that which is known.

TIN

Because of my misgivings about surfcasting in daylight, there is not as much that I can say about so-called "tin" lures. It has never been the custom to use these at night; consequently, my experience and success are more limited than with any of the other lure types in use. Origination of the term tin comes from when the material was more readily available in the early days of surf fishing, roughly the forties when I was but a small boy. The material was popular because of its low melting point and believed to be superior to anything else because of its dull sheen and ease in polishing. It is also alloyable with lead, which enabled home manufacturers to both stretch their tin supply and formulate different levels of sheen. In those days the highest possible silver flash wasn't thought to be necessarily better. I vividly recall being taught by an old-guard toolmaker/surfcaster that the level of tin in alloyed material could be determined by biting with one's teeth. High levels of tin crackle more.

Years ago such toolmakers (and I was well on my way to being one myself when I left industry to teach Industrial Arts) often fashioned the tools for casting their own creations. I have known some models that could be bent to facilitate a variety of actions and more often than not were polished with beach sand at the very spot where they were tested.

I witnessed the use of one such home-fashioned tin lure about a mile east of Race Point Station on Cape Cod. There was decent sea running late that morning, as the wind had quartered west/nor'west delightfully in time with a falling moon tide. Water was hauling heavy left to right off a point where a subsurface bar continued out. I didn't know the fellow, but he was drawing considerable attention because he was taking one big striper after another—in broad daylight! Moreover, whatever he was using was being cast a greater distance than was the custom, and he was slow about beginning his retrieve, allowing the thing to settle into the depths.

Upon examining his creation I learned that his tin lure was long and thin, about 5 inches, and I'll guess it weighed close to 4 ounces: a very castable sand-eel simulator indeed.

As the above example indicates, such metal lures do have the advantages of superior castability in a headwind; their depth can be controlled, providing options that often do not exist with other choices; the nomenclature of such lures allays any concerns you might have about fulcrums, which so harry plug anglers: straightening hooks; single hooks, which can be installed if not there already, take a better bite on a gamefish's jaw and can be removed more easily for either a safe release or a quick return to the action. Lastly, there are going to be *days* when the striper fishing is good, and some or all of the advantages outlined are going to be needed.

Modern lures are rarely fashioned of tin. Most are alloys of less expensive materials, which have been chromed or plated. Modern manufacturing techniques applied to what is available to today's surfcaster offer a worthy choice of effective lures.

BUCKTAIL JIGS

It would be interesting to know just how long the so-called "jig 'n' pig" of freshwater bass fishing has been in widespread use. We do recognize that the leadhead jig sweetened with a strip of pork rind is a formidable weapon in the arsenal of most sweet-water fishermen.

The reason we ask is that East Coast stripermen have been using bucktail jigs laced with pork rind for at least forty years. Moreover, based upon my foggy recollection of fishing for both largemouths and stripers back then, I strongly suspect that the method was used by eastern surfcasters first. Then, of course, I had no knowledge of what was being done nationally, but chances are that if folks were not jigging largemouths off the bottom in the fifties in New England, they probably were not doing it anywhere else. We deduce, therefore, that the technique's real start came from striper fishing. Thereafter it was copied, or simulated, by largemouth bass fishermen, or the method was simply born out of good sense in fresh water the same way that it came to be in salt. Certainly such parallel developments are not unusual in sportfishing.

Of course saltwater fishermen I knew never called it a jig 'n' pig. Ours was a bucktail and pork rind, which occasionally enjoyed the added sophistication of having the pig skin replaced with a strip of white supple squid, which surfcasters felt added some badly needed fish stink. With either strip of meat, the lure was popular because it cast well, sank to fish-killing depths, and was equipped with a very strong single hook. I'm still convinced that the best style of jig to use has

Bucktail jigs are nothing more than castable flys.

never changed over all those years: the No Alibi Smilin' Bill. We used so many that the things started showing up in counterfeit form, mass produced by rubber mold. Then and still you can find unpainted jig bodies in tackle shops for roughly 50 cents. All you have to do is wind on some bucktail, dip the thing to the windings in white paint, and paint in the red mouth and eyes. Later you can watch the bluefish chew up the thread windings. Jigs were the first "flies" that I ever tried.

Many of the boys used to experiment with different styles of jigs, bullet heads and such, but I always feared them as a compromise, because I'm still convinced that one of the virtues of the smiling-type body is that the mouth causes the lure to swim gently in fast current. (I used to quietly hacksaw mouths into the bullet heads that friends gave me.) The open jaws of the jig look like swimmer plates to me. Naturally, if you are to go to all the trouble of making up your own jigs, innovation ought to be hitting you between the eyes. My effort at that was to use black-dyed bucktail on the top and green along the sides; windings were covered with epoxy to keep the bluefish, which love them also, from wrecking the things; then I would paint in black and green on the jig head that was in harmony with the deer hair. Once dry it was easy to add the vermiculations (swiggles) of a mackerel with dark paint. What with a red mouth and pupils on the eyeballs, the thing looked pretty good. Nights on midwatch hunts for stripers, over cold whiskey or hot coffee, I used to love to spring one to the view of a trusted friend, swearing him to secrecy while he begged with delight for a little closer look.

The pork-rind part of the combination was always a source of consternation for me. The plain jig yielded an awful lot of stripers, and the jig with pork rind yielded an awful lot of stripers. Just when I would get the feeling that the "pig" wasn't needed, somebody would take a good fish with a 5-inch striper strip—as Uncle Josh calls it—and I would go back to carrying my little jar. Some of the New York City bunch that I fish Cape Cod with chip in for a whole pork belly, then slice it into strips with a razor. They actually fish with 12-inch striper strips. Getting your own pork bellies and lancing them into foot-long sweeteners may be carrying self-sufficiency too close to a charge of buckshot from the farmer down the road.

With or without the pork rind, the system's best application is in fast water that is too much for any other method. For example, a tidal marsh that fills and empties between a pair of jetties will, at midtide, sizzle and foam with moving water. Throw a plug into that, and it will skim ineffectively on the top. Toss a sinker and bait to the bottom, and the tide will sweep it away. Yet in spite of appearing to be too fast, too violent, and to hold water for stripers, it is the kind of structure that they truly love; never underestimate a bass's ability to hold in such turbulence. They do so by hugging the bottom or holding in the neutral hydro created by a rock. Moreover, they are not there to rest, but to wait patiently for something to drift by at whatever speed. Only a bucktail jig will get down to where they are; only a bucktail jig will ride hook up amid the clutter of the bottom, and only a strong single hook can withstand the forces generated by both great fish and mighty tides.

Avoid wire leaders while jigging, if you are serious about fishing for stripers. I can only speculate as to why, but the feeling that bass can either see or feel the wire on the take has always bothered me, because long ago I started catching more stripers when I dumped the wire.

One of my favorite jig-fishing places, one where I have moistened my brow many times on brute striped bass, has those kinds of tides. There I flip 9/0, 3-ounce jigs with 50-pound mono after selecting a spot where the rocks of the jetty offer a natural fighting chair. There are no give-and-take drag settings in this fishing. It is she or I as the leather of my drag washers comes out the side of the reel in a paste. With a falling tide to her advantage, one gets the true feel of power a 40-pound striper can exert.

As our freshwater counterparts have helped to prove, jigs will consistently take a large variety of gamefish in addition to stripers. We regularly catch bluefish with them, they are the best way to fish for weakfish, and, because of their weight, they fall right into the cod's kitchen. One autumn night years ago we caught stripers, blues, weakfish, and cod with the very same bucktail jig.

Much like tin, bucktail jigs offer the similar advantages of sinking, thus providing depth control. There is the aforementioned single-hook advantage. They may not cast quite as well as other metal lures, but they are a close second. Most importantly they work during either day or night, and most of the blitzes that I have had in the brightness of sunlight were with jigs.

PART FOUR

STRIPED BASS—
TRENDS, TRAITS,
AND BEHAVIOR

≈ Stripers Then and Now ≈

hat was it like in the good old days of striper fishing? Was the fishing better? Were there more big fish then?

These questions come up all the time when I meet new people to the surf, but they are too lacking in specifics for me to offer clear answers. For instance, *when* were the good old days, and how good were they? The answers depend, too, on who is being asked, and it is impossible to answer without first treating any number of considerations at considerable length and in detail. It is our purpose here to do just that, in offering a close examination of what fishing was then up to what it is now.

THE SIXTIES

Around 1959, before I had any interest in surf fishing, both boat and surf fishermen in Provincetown were catching an unusually large number of bass from 40 to 60 pounds. For them it was the best fishing in memory. That action died out by the early sixties at about the time that I started fishing the beach. I didn't know the catch dynamics of other classic places at that time, however. Then, say 1961, we were fishing small inlets with freshwater tackle for schoolies that were available at just about all the places that we fished. That year I had the top striper in our gang: 4¼ pounds! Of course, I'm certain that our tendency to catch small fish was related to both our methods and limited knowledge of striper hot spots.

Frank Woolner, editor emeritus of Salt Water Sportsman *magazine, and Curt Gowdy, veteran voice of the Boston Red Sox and former host of* American Sportsman, *talk striper fishing in 1958, when the surf was a new playground.*

In 1962 we enjoyed a blitz of bluefish in Charlestown, Rhode Island, that averaged 2 pounds, but one daybreak I landed a 10-pound lineside fishing squid on the bottom; it drew a crowd of curious surfcasters awaiting the dawn. Bluefish had caused considerable excitement at the time, as most people, including ourselves, had never seen them before. Nor did we see them again for a number of years.

My first big striper was a 17-pounder in 1964, and my second that year weighed 52. In those days there was better documentation of 50-pound-plus fish than there is now, because the R.J. Schaefer Salt Water Fishing Contest accepted entries from all anglers for fish of that size. That year between Maine and New Jersey, there were about two hundred such fish from boats and twenty-five from the surf.

During that time I started fishing Cape Cod's Nauset Beach, where fantastic numbers of schoolies were available. These averaged 6 pounds, and you could count on an occasional fish in the high teens. In my fishing club the top surf fish, all through the mid-sixties, was around 40 to 42 pounds, and there were not many. I hasten to add that in those days we commonly heard stories of people who had fished years before catching a striped bass.

The nature of my angling at the time was to fish the Cape for large numbers of school fish through July, then turn my efforts toward Rhode Island from August on. My feeling was that Rhody offered better opportunities for a truly big striper. We'll never know if these notions tended to fulfill their own prophecy, but I landed my next 50-plus in 1966 and another two in 1969 in Rhode Island. During that period Schaefer Brewery statistics for 50-pounders coastwide varied to as low as a hundred fish—surf and boat combined—but the percentage of surf-caught 50s remained constant at roughly 10 percent.

Two things were happening to muddy our perception of the fishing of the time: First, the bulk of the striper population was growing, and my own level of activity in the surf had increased to rabid levels. Growth in size and numbers of bass, however, can be extrapolated from Maryland young-of-the-year indices. These were highest during the sixties, with record viability levels right through 1970.

Commensurate with heretofore unknown levels of stripers was the rise in rod-and-reel commercial fishing. At the time there was no stigma attached to selling fish. Hauling a few bucks from the Atlantic was considered an honorable, almost agrarian, activity. With bass being bid on the floor of the Fulton Fish Market as kosher fish, prices climbed, creating greater incentives for stripermen to hound the species at a greater level than would be normal. The more fish people caught, the harder they worked at it. I was fishing the beach 130 nights per year, taking hundreds of stripers, but a bluefish was a rarity.

In 1969 I went to Block Island for bluefish after hearing about how well some club friends were doing with popping plugs from boats off Southeast Light. This may sound like a strange thing for a money fisherman to do, but the promise of high drama while fishing for a new species excited us. During that trip I landed around a dozen *monster* bluefish that ranged from 8 to just over 10 pounds. My first published story, "Block Island Safari" (*Salt Water Sportsman*, August 1970), lauded the place as number-one bluefish opportunity in the Northeast. I never could have anticipated that I would be surfcasting in Provincetown the very week the story came out and that regulars there—landing blues over 15 pounds every night—would read it and laugh. The notion of how little I knew about where to find good bluefishing hit home while admiring a 12-pounder that a towny had just slid up on the beach.

Interrupting my fishing to gaze at it, I remarked that it was a nice fish. The towny, trying not to swagger or ruffle sensitive feathers, said, "I've never seen one that small."

There was some comfort in the idea that the editorial staff of the largest international magazine devoted exclusively to saltwater fishing had known no more than I and that they could share in the error.

THE GLORY DAYS

The monster striper fishing of the good old days for us began in 1976 and held up through 1978. The Provincetown great blitz of '77 routinely provided nightly 40-pounders all through June and most of July until they disappeared late that month. The sprinkling of 50s probably numbered around fifteen for the entire area during that two-month period, during which surfcasters actually caught more stripers per hour than boat fishermen in the same vicinity.

We had slightly bigger fish a year later on the Cape, but the numbers were down somewhat and the writing on the wall forebode lean years to come. School bass were as rare as 40-pounders once had been.

From 1979 through 1986 the situation was one of decline, as traditionalists staggered through the motions of small isolated blitzes of occasionally outlandish-size stripers.

Most notable in my experience was the autumn blitz of '81 on Nauset Beach. Many parties of anglers fishing from the same buggy reportedly had numerous 50-pound-plus fish stacked side by side. I was never able to confirm these multiple 50-pounders, and with my knowledge of the common propensity to exaggerate, I doubt that as many were taken as was said. Still, I estimated that roughly sixty monsters were taken in a ten-day period, probably more such fish for any like period than ever before in the history of the striper surf.

Stephen Petri, of Lindenhurst, Long Island, aged seventeen, landed a 57 and delivered it to a taxidermist the next day. The following day he replaced it with a 69½!

The second weekend of that month, I landed five fish from 33 to 46 pounds. During the trip I met numerous people who had landed 50s in the course of the week, and I helped Andy Mendola, a New York City friend whom I had met in P-Town ten years before, beach a 60-pounder. Wally Brown, a local taxidermist, was given four other 60-pound-plus bass to mount in the same period. Late that season on Nauset, there was reportedly a 70-pound-plus lineside beached. It was, however, the end of glory-day striper fishing.

Of course, these experiences are meant to illustrate an image that would ideally represent a sampling of fishing of the time. No surfcaster, not even one who deluded himself into thinking that he was worthy of writing books on striper fishing, could know everything about every place.

Growth rates considered, we must now examine modern striper fishing in terms of the first Chesapeake year-class to signal recovery of the species: 1982. There had been a moderate success in 1978, but these fish were harvested before they could make any significant contribution to population levels. It was the 1982 year-class, however, that inspired heretofore unknown levels of regulation. Length limits moved above 16 inches for the first time in striper management history, sliding upward to 38 inches (18 pounds) by 1990. Where daily bag limits had been unknown, most striper states allowed one striper per day, while others allowed none. Commercial netting was banned, and the total of these actions became known as the moratorium. Even where conservative regulation permitted some commercial harvest, New York state banned the sale of bass because of PCB contamination, thus denying access to the largest fish market in the world.

From 1985 on striper anglers found themselves with a length limit that at first teetered on the edge of the size of most available fish. Later, once bass reached 32 inches in 1988, an increasingly larger percentage of the 1982 year-class was left unprotected by size limits that lagged behind growth. Utilizing the new measuring system of total length, anglers were finding bass just over the size requirement. At this writing we find ourselves with an unprecedented number of 18-to-20-pound stripers and enough bluefish—long a target of opportunity in the striper surf—available to keep things interesting.

Which year would you like to go back to? Nineteen sixty-two, when people ran down the beach excitedly to catch boiling schools of bluefish that weighed 2 pounds, and when big stripers were hard to come by? Shall I dial the time ma-

Charley Cinto, pictured here with a 73-pound behemoth he took in 1967, was the first of a long list of stripermen to top the 70-pound mark after fifty years of quiet.

chine to 1970, when sensational school striper fishing precluded any hope of an occasional weighable fish, and where you could catch blues either at Block Island or P-Town and never get another anywhere else?

Then? Now? Time plays tricks on us in our evaluation of these periods. First, we select the best year among twenty to compare with this one. Naturally, our mind is going to select something from out of the past that is better than what we have now. Merely raising the question implies the notion that people believe that things were better in the, ahem, good old days. Even then—and I make the remark without regard to year—people always complained about the fishing. Also, there are man-made or social considerations.

In the old days we had access to 45 miles of Cape Cod beach; now we have 7. Local people, operating under the guise of concern for the environment and endangered wildlife—have duped otherwise noble conservation groups into believing that fishing the beach was harmful to nesting shore birds and damaging to dune grass. Paid memberships work wonders.

The rod-and-reel commercial has gone the way of the buffalo hunter. I choose that analogy to underline that the uncontrolled hunter inevitably suffers the same fate as his quarry.

Lastly, let me draw you a picture. Supposing that the same people were permitted to keep all the stripers that they wanted over 16 inches, that they could bring them to the free market, and that beach access levels were returned to those prior to 1985. Here is what would happen. Numbers would keep fishing interesting, price would keep more people in the water for a longer time, and the larger fish—those thought to not even exist—would start showing up in the catches. Poundages would be high, income would create an inducement for fishermen to fish harder, and the results of such efforts would create unusual catches at times. Considering the numbers of undersize fish today, 500-pound catches would take place just as they did in the past, and, inflation considered, these would yield $2,000 nights. The times when fishing was bad, really a common occurrence for any type of fishing, would be forgotten. Ten years later people would call 1992 "the good old days."

Lastly, in an effort to acknowledge the inscrutable effects of time, don't we all wish we were what we used to be? These, patient reader, are the good old days!

⤙ World-record Striper: Does She Swim? ⤚

F ew striper fishermen would deny that the last ten years or so have yielded some historically enormous-size bass. I'm not talking about the reachable, now and then, 50-pounders that people you probably know have taken, however rare; I mean high 60s and up.

Digging into history is important here, because I do not believe that one's chances, however slim, have always been the same for taking a big bass. The number of such available fish is dependent upon the number born twenty-five years or so before, as well as their rate of survival. The first factor, spawning success, is fairly well known because of young-of-the-year surveys. Students of the species know that the sixties produced some of the greatest year-classes ever known. We can assume then that there ought to be more twenty-five-year-old fish than usual. Exactly how good survival of those sixties year-classes has been is quite another story, which admittedly tends to make this discussion somewhat speculative.

If we suppose for a moment that a few more fish of that midsixties era are around, then chances increase that the yield of Moby, 70-pound-plus fish are available. We hasten to add, however, that this is a long-shot discussion: For instance, your opportunities drop from one in ten million to one in one million, so put the camera away. All we are trying to point out here is that opportunities for world records have not remained historically constant. No better example exists than that of the Charles Church's 1913 World Record of 73 pounds. It held for sixty years without anyone even clearing the 70-pound mark to come close. Yet when it was broken, there had been a flurry of 70-pound-plus fish within the span of a decade. It is abundantly apparent that the late 1960s on had more 70-pounders for the catching.

Look at the record. Charley Cinto was first in 1967 with a 73-pounder taken at Cuttyhunk with a trolled Goo-Goo Eyes plug on wire line. Poor Charley, and I knew him well then, lost so much time weighing the thing that he and friends were certain that they would have topped Church. The fish failed to qualify for the world record consideration, however, because of wire line and trebles on the plug. Not long after, 1969, Ed Kirker of Fall River landed a Cuttyhunk lineside of 72 pounds on a live eel. Unaccountably, the International Game Fish Association (I.G.F.A.) ruled Kirker's fish a new record because Church's fish was put into question due to unsure tackle and weighing information, much to the dismay of many striper anglers.

Nevertheless, the flap over that was short-lived due to Bob Rocchetta's 76-pound fish, which cleared both Church and Kirker with a comfortable margin. Observers never figured on the present All-Tackle World Record of 78½ pounds, taken in the New Jersey surf by Albert McReynolds on a spinning rod with a Rebel. Point is that nothing came in for fifty years, then there were four 70-pound-plus stripers in a span of fifteen.

Maybe the strongest case, which shows how big a striper really gets, lies in an examination of some of the big linesides taken by commercial netters back when they were active. An Amagansett, Long Island, commercial fisherman, Ted Lester, haul-seined a 78-pounder, which was on display at a Montauk marina for years. All that before Church's record fell.

On the Cape at the Nauset Beach parking lot, there used to be a commemorative plaque honoring a 90-pound-plus bass that was taken in the late nineteenth century with a hand line by a surfcaster who whirled a cod drail over his head with the tackle of the time. Now that is surfcasting the hard way. There is supposed to be another off Orleans, Massachusetts— the same area—that scaled 112 pounds.

In January off the coast of North Carolina, it has long been known that huge bass lay into a staging area before spawning. There is reference to this in *Fishes of the Gulf of Maine* (Bigelow and Schroeder), where it is said that "several of about 125 pounds were taken . . . . [in] 1891." I read an account somewhere that there had been one in the seventies along with another over 100 pounds.

Gus Piazza, from Brooklyn, New York, sent me a beautiful letter years ago about an 81-pounder that he found on the floor of the Fulton Street Market where he worked in January 1967. I kind of felt that I knew him, because I had spent years with his brother Nate drinking spiked coffee on the tailgate of his buggy on Cape Cod. Anyway, Gus said that the shipment was from the south, probably North Carolina, and had a pair of 72-pounders along with the 81-pounder. He bought it for $20 and convinced the Schaefer Brewery people to mount it. After making the rounds of sports shows, it was sold for $1,000 to a New Jersey restaurant for display.

Lest you think that all we have is ancient history, January of 1988 the National Marine Fisheries Service conducted a tagging expedition between Corolla and Cape Lookout, North Carolina, where they trawled up 1,335 linesides. Their top fish was 65 pounds. Granted, this was not a record, but they didn't tag everything that was there either. What I have been trying to point out, fully conscious that talk of big fish is always interesting anyway, is that stripers grow way bigger than the ones that have been caught.

Growth charts indicate, though admittedly they get fuzzy at the top where less is known, that a world-record striper would be between twenty-five and thirty years old and would be certain to be a female. (Males rarely exceed 15 pounds and the largest known weighed 40.) If you count backward, any surviving fish from the burgeoning year-classes of the sixties might be at the threshold of world-record size in the early nineties with this possibility enduring until late in the decade.

It would be risky to downgrade today's striper fishing, where big fish are concerned, because the year-classes that would produce such a fish were, historically, the best ever recorded. Well-documented observations of striper population dynamics have shown a decline in reproduction since 1970. The culprit is over-fishing, since that might have jeopardized survival of the fish we speak of. Some would argue that the increase in 70-pounders caught in the last twenty years is indicative of that and others might testify that decline of younger fish has diverted attention away from striper fishing, inadvertently protecting older ones.

If the call is close, autumn stripers tend to be up to 10 percent larger than those of spring or early summer. Record fish tend to be outrageously girthy; moreover, if they have been feeding well hours prior to their landing, there is an additional weight advantage. Linesides 40 pounds will often hammer 3-pound hickory shad when feeding. Therefore, it is not outside the bounds of sound reasoning that future world records could edge themselves over the top simply on the strength of how they had been feeding.

I share the widely held belief that one's chances for a world record increase between Montauk and Cape Cod. And, if history is any teacher, it will be caught in a boat, where most of the larger fish have traditionally been taken. Admittedly, these are risky viewpoints when we acknowledge that Rocchetta's world record was boated west of Montauk; but my case thins even more when examining McReynolds's current New Jersey–caught world record, particularly in light of the fact that it was *surf* caught. But the reality that it was taken by a surfcaster is a greater celebration of fact for me than having been wrong all my life about where and how such a record may be caught.

Indeed, the McReynolds World Record inspires a pair of considerations here that fit the discussion. First, the International Game Fish Association (I.G.F.A.) makes no distinction between surf- and boat-caught fish of any species. Such "surf records" are mere statements of fact, not an effort to distinguish between boat and surf records, because there really are none. Secondly, most of the tackle in widespread boat fishing use is capable of handling the next record. But present-day surf tackle, at least that used most widely, is not likely to subdue a record lineside. McReynolds was using a spinning outfit, which implies line of no more than 20-pound test, flying in the face of my beliefs.

One of the disturbing things about the two most recent world records is that they may reflect the change occurring in striper population dynamics. Formerly scientists believed that 90 percent of East Coast bass came from the Chesapeake and that most of the remaining population was from the Hudson River. Chesapeake environmental decline, which took place at roughly the same time as environmental and conservation improvements on the Hudson—say throughout the seventies—caused a reversal in their roles whereby racial dominance between the two areas was exchanged. Today Hudson River fish are suspected of having the greater number. While Chesapeake fish are known to be highly migratory, those of the Hudson are believed to be less so, particularly the larger ones. Moreover, Hudson fish are exposed to less commercial netting, especially since the closure of haul-seining on Long Island and the traps in Rhode Island. In contrast entire year-classes of Chesapeake "rocks" have been wiped out to the south. If Hudson fish stray less distance from their mother river, and we look at the two largest bass taken in recent history—those of Rocchetta and McReynolds, from Long Island and New Jersey, respectively, which were both caught in summer not far from the Hudson—one cannot help but seek to establish a relationship between where they were caught and the river of origin. Emergence of the Hudson as the new dominant race of stripers is a plausible explanation for what might be a new trend in monster striper yields. The next great fish to come along could be pathologically examined for PCBs to determine their origin. The substance has been the "fingerprint" of Hudson fish since its discovery in the environment. If my theory is correct, there will be many more 70-pound-plus linesides taken from striper hot spots that break with tradition, and their origin will be the Hudson River.

SPEAKING OF SIZES

A number of factors will influence the weight of a given striper. This weight becomes a function of length and girth. While length naturally extends with age, and females usually outlive males, girth tends to follow seasonal lines. Spring or early-summer bass tend to be drawn down both from spawning and migration during a season when feeding opportunities have been leaner.

Fall stripers, on the other hand, probably have not been traveling as far in the waters of the striper coast. They have recovered of course from the rigors of their leanest season, feeding heartily all summer. And the sea in autumn is as much the lush garden of predatory opportunity as is the land. As a consequence most of the big fish that you will encounter will be well fed, and some will have gorged heavily on bait.

For the discussion to be complete, we must also take into account that there are variations in individual physiology where some fish tend to be slim, while others are more girthy in their natural build. Over the years I have heard of outlandish striper girths that raised the fish's weight and sent its appearance askew, but I have not seen many. Conversely, in the weighing of hundreds of big fish, including those of others, I have seen many particularly long and slim ones, usually called "racers," that should have weighed much more than they did. They often evoked a measure of outrage from the angler who engaged them in hard-fought battles. Experiences such as catching linesides over 50 inches long that weighed in the 40s when the surfcaster thought the fish should have weighed 50 pounds, or taking slim 50-pound-plus fish that with an appropriate girth would have scaled 60 pounds, had fishermen groaning about "the breaks" and kicking the tires of their buggy.

Still, the lion's share of big fish usually ends up being pretty average in their proportions. The commonly known rule of an inch per pound in stripers is quite accurate but limited to average-build fish right around the 50-pound mark. Way larger or smaller than that, the rule isn't any good as you'll see in the chart.

The widely known formula—length x girth (squared) divided by 800—is astoundingly accurate in determining striper weights of all sizes. You can test these with a calculator using the numbers I have.

As a fishing-contest weighmaster for ten years, I used a sealed scale on the beach and measured fish for the affidavits of anglers there. Except for duplications I logged striper measurements and weights that were the product of weighing hundreds of fish. From the yellowing pages of my old log book, which is jammed with fishing notes, here are some of the numbers:

Weight (lbs.)	Length (in.) *	Girth (in.)
15	34	19
18	38	19½
20	40	20
21	41	21
23	40	22
28	40½	24
37	44	25½
40	47½	25½
40	46½	25½
41	46½	26½
42	47	26¼
45	47	27
45	49	26½
46	49	26½
47	47	28½
50	50	27½
52	51	28
52	52	27½
52	50	29
54	52	28
55	52½	28¾

* = fork length

⤚ Releasing Stripers ⤙

One night you run into a concentration of stripers that provides the kind of fishing old-timers are always talking about, where nearly every cast yields a lineside. Only difference is that now, with conservative size limits, few of the fish are large enough to keep.

Late into the night it is one striper after another, each released gently into the surf, some more easily than others. Then at some point it is bound to occur to each angler: How many of these stripers are going to make it?

Naturally, the mortality of all released gamefish is dependent upon numbers and types of hooks used, size of fish, whether a bait or artificial is being used, where a fish is hooked, time played, time in hand, landing place, and even water temperature. Moreover, all of these variables can combine in a greater number of "sets" of variables to create different results. For instance, worst case, it is possible for an angler on a rocky shoreline to hook a large fish in the gills that causes bleeding; there may be several injury sites with treble hooks that require an inordinate amount of time for removal, the thing having bounced in the rocks while landing in a roaring surf. Under that set of conditions, it is unlikely that any striper would survive.

Sign of the times: Small stripers are the future of this great sport.

In thirty years of surfcasting for stripers (in addition to several other years when I knew little of what I was doing), I have been in dozens if not hundreds of striper blitz situations in which a great number of people were catching a lot of stripers that were being returned because of being undersized. I recall only one instance where a small fish washed up on the beach. That is not to say that some fish didn't die later and go undetected, but I truly believe that survival in most cases was nearly 100 percent. Moreover, there is considerable variability in the methods used for these experiences. They've included small, single-hook jigs on late April schoolies, fish taken on sea worms off the bottom, 14-inch linesides tangled in the treble hooks of plugs, and fly-caught bass that had no trouble gulping a wispy tuft of feathers.

But even that experience is incomplete because little is known of the effects of releasing LARGE stripers. With the size limits that are in place these days, many 16-pounders are being returned when what I learned about releasing fish was with 16-inchers! Today's throw-backs are thus ten times the size of those in years past.

Stripers that require two hands to hold while removing a hook present a different set of problems. It is not as easy to land 16-pound-plus linesides quickly to reduce fight time, the possibility of being injured increases, a big fish will take a hook or lure down deeply more quickly, and they are older and presumably less resilient to stress. A large striper is harder to handle, increasing the time the fish is out of water, greatly increasing mortality.

Conversely, big fish do not suffer the relative injury of those of their smaller counterparts. The wounds inflicted by a three-treble Finnish swimmer on big bass are more likely to be superficial than those inflicted upon a schoolie, where relative penetration is greater. It is easier to reach into the maw of a big fish to remove hooks than that of a small one where there is insufficient space for the hand. No question but that less is known of the release mortality of big bass.

Striper fishing can draw from any number of valid experiences from other species, however, in this age of widespread catch-and-release.

Trout fishermen, more often fishing with flies in private water, have long known that their fish could be caught more than once. The relatively recent widespread development of public catch-and-release trout waters has taken advantage of this fact. I submit that you will find few, if any, dead trout in such places where hundreds of fish are released a dozen times. Some salmon rivers, at least the ones I fish, have many more salmon released than killed. I have never seen one washed up on the bank. And Great Lakes tributary steelhead, more often released than not, have shown evidence of near-zero mortality from what I see.

Back to what we think we know about stripers. With the bass there is a dichotomy of techniques in widespread use. Unlike the trout and salmon examples above, which utilize flies or small hooks, linesides are taken with multiple hooks, large single hooks, baits, flies—you name it. Many methods no doubt suffer from a high mortality; you can't swim a live bunker with a 4/0 treble in his back, have a cow bass take it down, and then end up swallowing the thing. While most bass of the old days that fell for the aforementioned offer were keepers, it is not hard to envision an 18-pounder or more, which is going to be released, inhaling such a live bait. Then what? Many would tell you to cut the leader, but no studies have ever been made as to what happens to such a fish. Moreover, attitudes are different now, and a greater number of anglers are returning keepable linesides. We assume fishing methods have undergone some change that would be consistent with the new ethic.

A few tips on handling stripers for release: Never grasp a fish by the gills. These are a fish's lungs and damage easily. If there is any bleeding from the gills, that fish will most likely die. If water conditions permit keep the fish in the water as long as you can. The old-time idea that wetting the hands will help fish is no longer considered of major importance. Opponents of hand wetting feel that wet hands cause the angler to hold more tightly, which ends up causing more harm. Bait fishermen who deep hook and can't remove the hook quickly should cut the leader. Where plugs are used any hooks that can't be backed out easily should be cut out. Most superficial cuts will heal. Guiding considerations should be speed and the reduction of stress on the lineside.

BAY STATE MORTALITY STUDY

Massachusetts Marine Fisheries, with funding from the National Marine Fisheries Service, conducted an interesting hook-mortality study in 1989. They trucked one thousand small stripers that had been trapped in Rhode Island to a marine estuary in Salem, Massachusetts in late April. After a few months of acclimatization, some fifty anglers went to work fishing for them while technicians recorded information as to technique, tag date, anatomical hook site, handling, and time on the line. Because of the physical characteristics of the unique salt pond used in the study, officials were able to control outward migration to the sea, nonprogram fishing, and when finished, draw down the estuary for seining to ascertain striper survival.

Of 903 bass in the final hooking study, two groups were established: 688 that were never landed and 215 that were. That fall, upon conclusion of the study, 198 of the caught fish were alive in the pond, indicating a mortality of 17 fish, or 8 percent. Interestingly, about 8 percent of those bass never caught were also missing, which suggests a background or natural mortality similar to that of those that had suffered various hooking injuries. While the data from the research is final, analysis is still tentative at this writing.

I surmise from reading the preliminary data that 8 percent mortality would be the high end of the true result. Also, there was the observation that many fish landed with single-hook jigs had deeper, more severe injuries than those caught with multiple-treble hooks. The latter tended to inflict many superficial wounds but less penetration.

These were small bass averaging 13 to 14 inches and weighing roughly 1 pound, 2 ounces, which would exacerbate the injury inflicted by a relatively large single hook. We hasten to add that size of fish involved may not serve all the purposes of this discussion. But it does indeed support the contention that releasing linesides is far from any waste.

Nonetheless the study, "Estimating Mortality of Hooked and Released Striped Bass," carried out by Marine Fisheries biologist Paul Diodati, certainly is the first of this kind that I know of and most welcome in these days of striper commitment and widespread concern. Moreover, it confirms something that we have long suspected: Hooking mortality with small linesides, even though varying with method, is slight.

☙ Water: Quality and Temperature ☙

T he pollutants that foul the striper's rivers of origin read like a chemist's shopping list. The Chesapeake rivers, as well as others to the south, which we tend to lump together as "Chesapeake," contain less organic pollution but more pesticides and herbicides as runoff from intense farming activity. It remains unproven just how much these hazardous materials have influenced striper populations, but these are believed to be the cause of recent loss of viability: the ability to reproduce. Add to these the highly suspect acid rain, and you have a compendium of suspected causes either of juvenile mortality or failure to produce successfully hatched out year-classes of stripers.

The Hudson River, on the other hand, suffers more organic pollution in which poorly or untreated sewage fouls its waters at a level that raises questions about the future of the species. PCBs, which have been in the river's sediments for dozens of years, are still being found in trace amounts of striper flesh varying from 2 parts-per-million (ppm) to 100 ppm. PCBs are *suspected* to be a carcinogen for man, but this has never been proven. Public health officials nevertheless have reduced the allowable levels of PCBs from 4 ppm to 2 ppm, rendering Hudson stripers unfit for consumption. Two things should be said about this: 1) The true hazardous level of PCBs that should be allowed for human consumption is an arbitrary figure; and b) This reduced tolerance for the contaminant has served to protect all migrating stripers from the commercial marketplace to the species' recovery advantage.

In spite of high contamination levels in Hudson stripers, the presence of PCBs has not had a deleterious effect upon the species. Indeed, Hudson stripers have prospered in spite of, even because of, politically, the presence of PCBs.

When we take into account that year-class after year-class of spawning stripers have been successful there, a picture emerges of the species being remarkably resilient to both organic pollution and PCBs. It is not difficult to envision stripers wallowing in effluvium clouds of muck and goo. Those surf-casting friends of mine who live in New York City tell me that Hudson striper fishing has been reliable over the years and often better than the classic hot spots about which we so often read. While lamenting the striper decline of the early eighties elsewhere, these people never suffered one in the scuzzy, Love Canalish, home environment.

Away from the Hudson it has long been known that polluted rivers did little to repel stripers. Boston Harbor, the Providence River, New Haven—all places that a fish with a choice would ordinarily bypass—appeal to bass if the feeding opportunities are favorable.

All this discussion on the Hudson is not intended to shift emphasis away from the Chesapeake race of fish. It is simply a reflection of what is known of the Hudson.

WATER TEMPERATURE

Most regular striper anglers rely upon the calendar to tell them when they ought to begin and end their season. This works out pretty well for spring fishing most years, because the year-to-year early temperatures occur at roughly the same time for a given locale. In southern New England waters, say

Montauk to Monomoy, small bass can be counted upon to show up around April 25 and the big fish about a month later. To better make that determination, however, you can use seawater temperatures to determine the presence or feeding interest of stripers. The common denominator for such arrivals is a water temperature of 50 degrees F.

When I first started striper fishing, I used to wait for the first fish every spring, diligently taking the water temperature while baited lines sat motionless. I never once took a bass while reading 48 or 49. Just a couple of nights later, I wouldn't be able to keep bait on the hook, as small fish were jiggling the rod tips like mad. To my astonishment the water temperature would be "clicked over" the magic 50-degree mark. It was an experience that repeated itself during numerous early seasons. Many nights, midwatch nights when I stared at the rod tips against a starlit sky, I would wonder if the fish had been there all along, not taking until the temperature was right; or did the favorable water trigger their arrival? Maybe it doesn't matter, because our only concern is that the linesides are ready to be fished.

I am convinced that there are behavioral differences between Hudson and Chesapeake stripers that relate to adaptability to water temperature. No doubt the Hudson fish, hailing from farther north, have adapted to accept colder water temperatures when compared to their Chesapeake counterpart, which migrate later. During the striper shortages of the last ten years, there has been little discernible absence of small fish in spring, because early migrants were apparently of the more numerous Hudson River strain. During that period of the shift in dominance from Chesapeake to Hudson fish, the latter a virtual explosion, our dominant race of fish—with its cold-water affinity—changed, lengthening the season at both ends. If there is any accuracy in this, the observation comes out of fall fishing. Spring fishing remains unchanged, but that could be because we were always fishing Hudson linesides in the first place. We never cared.

For all fish there is a range of water temperatures at which that species will function best and be most likely to actively feed. We are certain that 50 is the low-point barrier for bass, but do not have the foggiest notion what the high point is. We doubt that ocean water north and east of Montauk ever gets too warm, because coastal southern New England waters rarely rise above 72 degrees F. And between 50 and 72, I have never observed any difference in feeding behavior.

Autumn striper-departure timing is a different story, because the conditions influencing sea-water temperatures are more varied. At some point in fall, the water reflects the total temperature conditions of previous months. That is, if it has been an unusually hot summer, fall temperatures start warm and are more able to resist cooling influences. Naturally, if these cooling factors are moderate, unfavorable water is delayed. Another point of physical law that has to be taken into account is that the water's mass does not respond quickly to air temperature; rather, it takes a prolonged period of cold to exert enough influence to draw down the temperature. This lag between air and water temperatures, which is at least a month, often finds us casting in 60-degree water with the air in the 30s, the seas steaming from their resistance to change. Unlike spring, when water has been resisting the freezing point all winter, there is more room for change before the critical departure temperature boots bass out of the territory.

Early season water only has to climb about 12 degrees from its low point, and autumn water has to fall more than 20 degrees. Naturally, this takes longer, slowing the period of sea change, making the departure of stripers far less predictable than their spring arrival. Season's end, measured as when bass are gone, varies as much as a month.

You can see the progression of departure moving down the coast by watching the fishing reports. Poor fishing will be reported at say, Saco, Maine, while striper anglers 100 miles to the south are cleaning up. That is one of those dangerous generalizations, however, that does not take social, or man-related, behavior into account. Very often people stop fishing because it is time to stop fishing, according to their calendar.

(Though I do confess to allowing the hunting season to end my fishing prematurely some years.) Life bears hard choices.

No question but that temperature of sea water should be the guiding consideration, a thermometer no small part of your equipment when beginning or ending the seasons. The theory that migration, in either direction, is triggered by the length of day or hours of daylight may be interesting as well as exhibiting some pretty good understanding of natural law; however, my experience does not accept it, though I admit that with my contentions I make no more forceful an argument than do those who advance light as the reason.

⟨ *Migration* ⟩

F all is when classic fishing presents itself in blitz proportions. This is when the sea, it seems, has bait at the greatest level. It is also the time when these bait fish are often
corralled against the shore taking a pasting, mostly from bass
and blues and sometimes from cod, pollock, and weakfish. For
most of us the season conjures visions of wheeling and diving
shorebirds with surfcasters below hurling lures into a wind-
whipped sea.

It is a major event in the natural scheme of things, because
hungry gamefish that must store energy both for travel and
endurance for the lean winter are far less choosy about what
they hit. Rare are the mysterious, little rubs of a fish turning
away from your plug or the halfhearted takes that we all recall
from summer. It's fishing time for locals and inland regulars
who have been saving vacations. For that reason timing is no
small part of the fisherman's bet. On average early October
will witness an increase in feeding activity on the southern
New England coast as well as offshore islands. To the north,
above Cape Cod, all gamefish will be schooled and moving.

Peak periods are no sudden flash of activity that ends that
quickly. Indeed, fall fishing for stripers and blues can be excellent for weeks. Good strategy dictates that northern sections,
Maine down to the Massachusetts north shore, will explode

first. Then as the season progresses, you can expect things to improve more to the south. Usually by mid-October the Cape's Race Point is the bonanza, and by November 1 Rhode Island anglers are wondering where all the fish came from. For many these dates may seem on the late side, and truly there might be some years when fall frosts arrive early. But over the long haul, I view them as the center of averages. Moreover, my experience has been that many regulars quit far too early because they started too early. One year while I was water-fowling in the Cape's Pleasant Bay in early December, 30- and 40-pound bass were working in bait. Another extreme example is the fall that Charlestown, Rhode Island, was red-hot over Thanksgiving weekend continuing into early December. We had snow flurries twice that week, but what makes that time stick in my memory was that all the regulars had gone to Cape Hatteras, hundreds of miles south, and found nothing.

Air and water temperatures seem to be the key. I'm not sure of the reason, but there is a 10-degree difference in the water on the two sides of an imaginary line drawn between Monomoy on Cape Cod and Nantucket. West of that line suitable temperatures, say above 50, hold so much later that the marine climate is dramatically different. Thus, while the Outer Cape would be a poor bet in November most years, Cuttyhunk, offshore islands, and Rhode Island might still be holding up quite well. And again it also depends on how cold the fall has been and what has happened to water temperatures. Some years we've bathed in Charlestown surf during Columbus Day weekend in 65-degree water, a full 10 degrees warmer than that found on the Outer Cape in August.

Of course, we need to consider other influences upon migratory patterns. Each species' temperature requirements vary, inspiring an order of departure: summer flounder, weakfish, blues, then bass. Cod are moving inshore. An important thing that can be inferred from that list, something fishermen have always known, is that if bluefish are still around, you can be certain that bass fishing isn't over.

Bait is needed in an area to both stop and hold the species

we fish for. Otherwise hungry, moving fish will pass an area by. How long they stay depends upon a mix of many factors that are hard for any angler to read. Severe line storms, which are in season at this time, can spell the end to any migration-inspired blitz. October and November are hurricane season, and storms of that intensity not only close the fishing, but leave the water too roily with suspended sand and weed stirred from the bottom for up to a week. Even the storms that miss us and pass offshore kick up a dangerous surf. But once things settle down, good fall fishing usually returns—if there is time left.

Major staging areas, classic strongholds for stripers and blues, will load up with fish and fishermen during the migration. All of these are places where ocean currents collide carrying bait, enhancing feeding opportunities. Such sizzling spots as Cape Cod's Race Point, narrows between the islands of the Elizabeth Chain (Cuttyhunk), the Cape Cod Canal, and Montauk will always lure New England fishermen in the know, because they hold the moving water that stripers and blues love. We hasten to add that for each of the major ones, the map is dotted with a hundred tiderips that are cumulatively as important. Places like Cape Cod's Chatham Inlet, and a myriad of small rivers on the southern New England coast come to mind quickly enough for us to avoid a distracting peek at the map.

I'm convinced that today's striper migration comes off later than it did years ago. Back in the so-called golden days of bass fishing, the big fish of the Cape would leave and never be heard from again. Now it seems as though they more often show up in Rhode Island in the late fall, say November; in recent years there have been outrageous blitzes on Block Island at that time. It is as though we were fishing for a different race of fish, a slightly different species. I can't be sure if my mind fabricates this knowing that many more of our stripers now come from the Hudson River, whereas the bass of earlier times came from the Chesapeake. Or are there in fact behavioral differences in the two strains of linesides? We can be sure that more bass are Hudson fish, and that when we fish for them we are fishing closer to where they are going. But the last inscrutable consideration—Do Hudson fish migrate later?—remains impossible to prove, because too little was learned when we had enough Chesapeake fish to count them. Moreover, we now feel that we have a better hold upon when we should be fishing than we did years ago. So much for unsubstantiated theory.

Certainly if there is a season when we can catch a lot of fish in the daytime, it is fall. Still, given a choice about when to make my casts, I would choose the same darkened hours that have sustained me throughout the season. I recall many times when Butch Calkins, an old surf comrade, my brother, Norman, and I caught so many big fish in the cold and bitter deep night on eels in Charlestown when it seemed that the world was waiting to drive the beach at daybreak. Indeed, had they ever found fish, there scarcely would have been room to cast for the number of people betting on the dawn. When you think of all the things you can do in the outdoors, isn't it a blessing that surfcasting is the one that can continue, day or night, until you drop.

Perhaps the best test of when the season is finished is when somebody lands a big, old codfish on a plug, a sure sign that the sea is cooling enough for them to be moving in from the offshore depths. It always happens at about the time that we begin to savor what it must have been like back before the nets and a million other fishing lines. When a mile of beach either way is devoid of all other fishermen, with no boats on the outside, there is something cozy and naturally tranquil, even at the moment when something is trying to take the rod from your hands.

⇒ *Efficient Hunters* ⇐

Man has a strong tendency to view striper behavior in human terms, applying the use of our senses to those of stripers. No doubt there is some accuracy in that application where the eye is involved. Certainly our fishing tells us that all fish can see. But what does a fish see, and how well does he see it? How efficient, in human terms, is its ability to smell? What and how does it feel?

Study of other animals tells us that their senses are different than ours, where some see better than we do; others have higher scenting abilities and some lower. To compound the difficulty of fully understanding our quarry, we not only fail to fully comprehend their senses in human terms, but we cannot fully understand their senses in so foreign an environment as water.

There is widespread belief in scientific circles that the lateral line present on most fish is a sort of biological sonar, which is able to emit an electronic impulse used in both sensing danger and foraging. The lateral line is present on all salmonids, cod, pollock, and haddock, to name those that easily come to mind. When this "sonar" is added to those senses that we both experience ourselves as a species and understand as observers, it becomes a totality of senses, which we had best call a proximity sense. While this new sense still is not fully explainable, we do know that stripers are capable of finding an artificial on the darkest night. When first locating it they cannot smell it, because it has no apparent scent. They are not touching it upon first discovery, and, presumably, it is too dark for them to see it at the distances that they often alter course for the chase. *Proximity* might thus best be thought of here as a total greater than the sum of sound, sight, and smell that the species might have at its calling. However we seek to explain it, much is thought to come from the lateral line—and the striped bass has six of them!

JUMPERS

One of the oldest friendly disagreements about bass that comes up among surfcasters is whether or not they jump. All agree that they slosh the surface, roll, pop, and throw water all over, but those calendar leaps of jumping clear, as with salmon and bluefish, are rare in my experience. Still, every now and then they will leap clear of the surface.

Around thirty years ago an early surfcasting mentor of mine took me to the Cape Cod Canal for the first time, saying that when the bass come out of the ditch for whiting it would sound like someone had thrown a mule off the Sagamore Bridge. We had one lineside exhibit the performance he promised during the dull gray of dawn: It was a sight that no shore fisherman would be likely to forget. An outlandishly large striper, it tail-walked a full 20 yards, pounding the surface several times as it went. Seeing it clearly as it raised that kind of commotion at the center of the canal, we estimated that it weighed somewhere between 40 and 70 pounds!

Ten years and hundreds of stripers later, we were fishing Provincetown's Second Rip one daybreak when linesides came up leaping all over the rip. We could tell that they were chasing something. Exactly why they leaped in their efforts to seize it, or why they also leaped when hooked on plugs, was

something that none of us there could understand. If it was the kind of bait that provoked this activity, why did they jump clear out when fast to a plug? Why did these particular fish have the jumps when those we caught previous nights and so many nights after did not? Stripers usually don't jump, but they did those times.

NATURAL NOVOCAINE

One night when a bunch of us were working a tiderip on the Cape, I noticed that some of the gang were fanning on strikes. After a while this began to evoke discussion as to what was bunting the plugs but was never there when casters hauled back after the take. I felt it, too. Your plug would drum in the tide, you would feel a whack, haul back in response, but there would be nothing there. People were still nearly falling backward with limp lines when George Carlezon, who cast left-handed so that we could stand shoulder to shoulder to breeze while fishing, whispered to me after landing his third, "Drop your tip and wait after the drum."

It takes a lot of discipline to do nothing when something punches your lure like that, but on the next encounter I waited, and sure enough, the drum was followed by a solid take. What we had all been doing was pulling the plug away from the taking striper.

The experience inspires two questions: What were they doing? And why do they suddenly exhibit such *uniform behavior* when it is a mode of taking that is seldom exhibited? How could we envision what was taking place on the end of a long cast in the deep night?

We all know that many forms of wildlife enjoy numerous predatory/survival adaptations developed through centuries of natural selection. The cats will break the spine of their prey quickly; deer, so often a part of some other creatures' solution, will graze with larger livestock, yet bolt at the scent of a carnivore; marlin and sailfish will spear their prey, then come around and pick it up. Could the stripers on the night in question have been doing something to the bait—in this case our plugs—that they thought allowed them to come around again and pick them up? Is it a plausible theory that this bang-and-bite behavior was first a killing blow followed by a marlinlike turn and take? Could they have been inflicting an injury with their dorsal first?

My attention goes to the dorsal fin, because I am convinced that the spines on the top of the bass are equipped with some sort of natural anesthetic. Bait fish so stricken drift helplessly from the stuff after being stabbed, then the bass just circles back in the next seconds to draw it in without having to worry about it escaping. I suspect that such natural anesthetic substance exists, because once while removing my eel from a fish, I knelt too close to the dorsal of a lineside, and it penetrated my knee slightly. When I got up to walk, my leg was dead, numb in a 4-inch circle to the point where you could have pushed needles into the skin without my feeling it.

Years ago my brother, Norman, kicked high and dry a 22-pounder that he had dropped in the wash. Quite proud of his successful act of desperation at first, he later complained of a leaking boot that he thought was full of water. Because there was no pain in his foot, he never dreamed the boot was filled with blood. Next day a 2-inch length of striper dorsal was surgically removed.

Drifting a plug from a Rhode Island jetty, I recall having it drummed but not hooking any fish unless the lure was left for the take seconds later. During live-eel fishing I've often, though not always, noticed a sharp drum on the strike. With free spooling a take, however, you would not know at exactly what point the bass had engulfed the eel. While live-eel fishing the night before this writing, my wife, Joyce, foul-hooked a 15ish-pounder with a single hook just 2 inches ahead of the dorsal. We have, in fact, foul-hooked many linesides right at or slightly ahead of the dorsal.

My case is not airtight. True, a certain amount of foul-hooking takes place in all fishing. Moreover, my theory could be merely half right, where the spearing occurs and the "novocaine" does not.

When we take into account the importance of this species, so little is known, and so much remains that should be explained. After a lifetime of striper fishing, the species remains a mystery to me, turning up in strange places, exhibiting erratic behavior. That may explain, at least in part, the charm of striper fishing and the Zen of surfcasting for it.

≈ *Index* ≈

≈ *About the Author* ≈

Frank Daignault's articles have been appearing in national and regional outdoor publications since 1970. While most of his writing has dealt specifically with surfcasting for stripers, he has published widely on fly fishing for trout and salmon, as well as upland hunting.

Daignault has lectured on fishing and hunting for outdoor exhibitions and sportsmen's clubs since 1979. As a member of the New England Outdoor Writers Association, he was honored in 1983 by the Daiwa Corporation for his encouragement of youth fishing. In 1990 both the Outdoor Writers of America and New England Outdoor Writers presented him with awards for writing excellence for an article that appeared in *Salt Water Sportsman* magazine.

Daignault lives with his wife, Joyce, in Blackstone, Massachusetts.